President Zine El Abidine Ben Ali of Tunisia

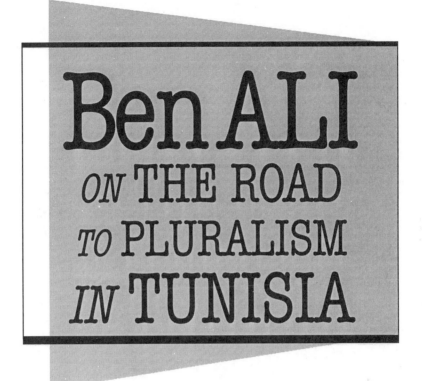

Ben ALI
ON THE ROAD
TO PLURALISM
IN TUNISIA

SADOK CHAABANE
Director General of the Tunisian
Institute for Strategic Studies

American Educational Trust
P.O. Box 53062
Washington, DC 20009
1997

ABOUT THE AUTHOR: Sadok Chaabane has a doctorate in public law and political science. Former Professor at the University of Tunis, Secretary of State, Counselor to the President of the Republic, and Minister of Justice, Dr. Chaabane is currently Director General of the Tunisian Institute for Strategic Studies.

This book was originally published in 1995 by Ceres Editions, Tunisia, in Arabic under the title *Ben Ali Wattarik ila Attaadoudia* and in French under the title *Ben Ali et la Voie Pluraliste en Tunisie*.

Chaabane, Sadok
  Ben Ali on the road to pluralism in Tunisia / by Sadok Chaabane.
    p. cm.
  Includes bibliographical references and index.
  ISBN 0-937165-07-7
  1. Pluralism (Social sciences)—Tunisia. 2. Democracy—Tunisia.
  3. Political participation—Tunisia. 4. Tunisia—Politics and
  government. 5. Bin 'Ali, Zayn al-'Ābidin. 1. Title.
  JQ3336.C43 1997
  323'.042'0961109049–dc21   97-37520
                                                              CIP

TABLE OF CONTENTS

LAYING THE GROUND:
Ben Ali's Approach to Democratization

The Complex Transition from Autocracy to Pluralism

THIS BOOK SEEKS to describe Tunisia's road to pluralism today. It examines the country's transition to pluralism after several decades of autocratic rule. Although it focuses on Tunisia's experience since President Zine El Abidine Ben Ali's accession to power on November 7, 1987, the book attempts to bring out the theoretical underpinnings of this approach and to describe the fundamental tenets of the country's political experience. The latter is compared to comparable, contemporary experiences of other countries in the Mediterranean region and other parts of the world.

Drawing upon the experience of my own direct involvement in political life since the 1987 transition, and using the personal vantage point from which I was able to witness the complexities of national reform, I have moved back and forth between theory and practice, ultimately comparing the policies of President Ben Ali to the academic paradigms of political change[1] which I was accustomed to discussing at the University.

The question is often posed by foreign and domestic observers as to the reasons Tunisia's pluralistic approach has succeeded, where others failed, in reconciling the imperatives of security with those of sustained growth. To answer such questions, I will search for the theoretical bases of Ben Ali's policies and for the patterns directing his major decisions. From this exercise, we will come to perceive the clear outlines of a comprehensive vision which is gradually and prudently being implemented by the President.

In adopting a pluralistic political model, Ben Ali opted for a particular orientation aimed at laying the ground for a pluralistic alternative and filling the political vacuum left by the previous regime. This book will seek to explain this orientation and point out its theoretical bases.

To my knowledge, analysts and theoreticians have not yet offered an adequate discussion of this particular approach to democratization. I have felt it useful,

1

therefore, to outline the main features of this model and leave it for others to further define its precise features. As a full-fledged theory of governance, this model could serve as a source of inspiration for policy-makers and politicians in the discussion of situations similar to those faced by Tunisia in the course of its journey toward democracy.[2]

First of all, one has to address the issue of laying the groundwork for the pluralistic alternative and filling the inherited political vacuum. The picture becomes clearer once one examines further the transition from autocratic rule to pluralism. The vacuum is created by the absence of democratic opposition. Pluralism cannot grow or last in the absence of an institutional, open and organized democracy which functions in a climate of harmony. Without this form of opposition, pluralism in emerging democracies is faced with the risk of relapsing into the previous state of autocratic rule, or of being thrown into another, more vicious, autocratic rule based on religious, racial or other forms of extremism.[3]

Hence it is imperative that the vacuum left by the previous autocratic rule be filled, and that a healthy democratic opposition be established. This is quite an arduous task. Contrary to what some are tempted to believe, the construction of institutional democracy is more difficult than resisting the threat from fanatical extremist movements. Such movements grow underground under autocratic rule. After the collapse of that kind of rule, they emerge and try to exert their domination over the new regime. The establishment of a democratic opposition depends not only on the amendment of legislation and the acceptance of criticism and differences. It also requires a degree of adjustment and training, the creation of a new spirit of competition between the opposition parties as well as within the majority party itself.[4]

This is the essence of the experience that Tunisians are going through today. The building of democratic opposition is the most delicate part of the journey toward pluralism. It is more sensitive and more critical than the fight against fanaticism and extremism, the defense of civil society, and the search for a consensus. There are many delicate balances which have to be preserved in any overturning of the political system. Democracy has to be the beneficiary in any such opening, not extremist movements which appear in full force immediately after the political change and try to steer the course of events in their direction.[5]

In the case of Tunisia, the pluralistic process began in an international setting that was hardly favorable. In the early eighties, Tunisia was among the very first countries to embark on this process. At that time, not many in the world were really aware of the danger of fundamentalism and its double-talk, nor were they conscious of the risks posed by the return of ultra-nationalism and the rise of the radical right, which caused a shift of the moderate right toward extremism and a severe weakening of the left.

The Establishment of Democracy in an Unsettled World

Major transformations took place on the world scene during the last decade. Certain regimes utterly collapsed while others emerged. Alliances and balances changed. Not enough attention was given by political analysts to certain profound changes which occurred during these years.

Political analysis focused on the collapse of the Communist Bloc and its impact on the traditional balance which had typified the world order since the end of World War II. A major theme was the triumph of capitalism and liberalism as systems of thought and political and economic organization. Market economic systems, including their more humanistic and rational variations, have come to be perceived as the only course of development. Democracy has become the ideology of governments from East to West. It has also been adopted as a yardstick of political progress and as a universal value espoused and promoted by great powers.[6]

During the last decade ample attention was given to the policies of *Perestroika* and *Glasnost* promoted by Soviet leader Mikhail Gorbachev, with the purpose of preparing the Soviet Union for a better future by endowing it with more adequate socio-economic structures and new value systems based on freedom and democracy. His objective was to build the Soviet Union's claim to greatness on new foundations. He wanted to give political life more transparency even if it meant uncovering the pervasive flaws which plagued the socialist system under the veneer of the much heralded successes. He aimed at liberalizing the systems of production and government in order to give more strength and credibility to the Soviet Union. His vision was the subject of both scrutiny and admiration in the West. With the exception of the reservations of some strategists, the consensus was that the Soviet Union would cease being a source of hostility in the future.[7] What was not predicted, however, was that Gorbachev would quickly lose control and that the Soviet Union would so totally unravel, allowing the former Communist countries of Eastern Europe to rid themselves of the yoke of autocracy and opt for a return to the values of free-market competition.

Another phenomenon was simultaneously taking place within and beyond the socialist countries, but attracting much less attention. That phenomenon, which marked a whole decade before and after *Perestroika*, was the demise of autocracy regardless of its ideological hue. Observers failed also to pay adequate attention to a concomitant trend, i.e., the return of nationalism. That trend manifested itself in the form of a quest for identity, and a hostility to Western civilization. In this regard, I differ with the point of view which claims that the demise of socialism has sealed the fate of all ideologies and opened the way for the prevalence of liberalism as a single unrivaled model. What has happened is slightly different. It is the appearance of a more dangerous ideological confrontation based on cultural and civilizational differences. Ethnic and religious nationalisms emerged as a threat to the world community. This trend manifested itself in the Soviet Union and Eastern Europe as well as in the Mediterranean region. In as much as it promoted ethnic confrontation and religious bigotry, it constituted a real danger to peaceful co-existence.[8]

Such trends prevented many emerging democracies from making any serious advances toward democratization. The struggle against autocracy quickly became a struggle against other cultures and civilizations. The drive for liberalization turned into a radical quest for identity. Faced with extremist movements they could not restrain, pent-up frustrations that were fast overflowing, and with unbridled ambitions and aspirations they could not channel in any healthy direction, certain regimes strayed off-course. Transition was no longer synonymous with reform and openness. The fight against autocracy was no longer a struggle for democracy and pluralism in a nationalist setting. It became instead a conflict pitting one religion against the other or an ethnic group against the other. [9]

Tunisia itself went through such a stormy stage. A lot of resentment and turmoil simmered underneath the surface of its previous autocratic regime. This was the breeding ground for extremist movements whose totalitarian agenda called for the overhaul of the existing model of society and the establishment of a more pernicious autocratic system based on theocratic rule. Such a form of government would base its legitimacy on confrontation with the West and the rejection of democratic and liberal values as symbols of Western domination. Aware of such risks, Ben Ali acted pre-emptively against the inherent dangers. He laid the ground for pluralism but closed the door in the face of extremist movements and violent fanatics. A key tenet of his approach was to allow for a gradual participation of the democratic opposition in the political process without giving radical movements, including fundamentalist groups, the chance of taking advantage of the emerging democratic system.

New Ideological Strife and the Return of Ethnic and Sectarian Movements

Racial and ethnic tendencies greatly increased their appeal, as the previous ideological polarization between socialist and liberal camps lost its mobilizing power, domestically and internationally.

Ultra-right currents grew steadily during the last three decades. Their extremist incarnations manifested themselves in the midst of the traditionally democratic countries of Europe, among others. Hence, neo-Nazi groups emerged in Germany. The National Front attracted a sizable following in France. Similar trends developed in Italy, Austria, Spain, Britain and other nations. The emergence of such movements caused a shift to the right by centrist parties which sought to re-position themselves in a manner that attract the votes of the new right. The steady decline of the left disrupted the existing political balance. Extremist fundamentalist movements came into existence in the Mediterranean region and elsewhere. What these movements had in common was bigotry and hatred of others. Much like racist movements, such tendencies are based on intolerance of differences, the distaste for democracy and the yearning for a totalitarian system of government that is more pernicious than that of socialist-type one party rule.

The sudden demise of communism led to the growth of nationalist movements. The collapse of the Soviet Union created a void soon filled with hate and rancor. Andrei Gratchen has offered the best analysis of this.[10] Gratchen argues

4

that instead of opening the way for new democracies, the Soviet Union was succeeded by states that were not more democratic. From within the communist establishment emerged leaders with a nationalistic message. For the first time, conflicts erupted between Russians and Ukrainians, with their newly erected borders. Abkhazis also battled Georgians. The economies of Eastern Europe were upset by the acute conflicts between the countries of the region. This situation led to an exodus to Western Europe, which stimulated the growth of nationalist sentiments by way of reaction.

Because of the lack of structured public opinion and clearly-defined political forces, populist movements can stir up raw nationalistic and religious sentiments by playing up certain slogans.

Fundamentalist movements in the Middle East and North Africa were able to tap into pan-Arabist sentiments and to use their political slogans for mobilization purposes. At the end of the eighties, some felt that fundamentalism might offer a haven for the discontented and an alternative for those seeking to defend Arab pride against Western domination. Fundamentalist leaders took advantage of the failures of pan-Arabism to co-opt the message of this ideology and appeal to its constituency. The tactic of the fundamentalists, as well as their double-edged rhetoric, became very clear during the Gulf war. Certain Baathist or Nasserite-led governments tried to strike an alliance with fundamentalist movements in order to gain the support of these movements' sympathizers for their own agendas. But they quickly abandoned this approach, or at least opted for a more prudent attitude, after discovering that these movements aimed for the same objectives. They saw that, despite their double-talk and deliberate ambiguities, these fundamentalist movements wanted only to gain more support and legitimacy for themselves.

Ideologically, there is therefore little difference between fundamentalist movements and ultra-nationalist movements. Both base their message not on reason, but on the appeal to faith and sentiment. Both also promote a belief-system that leaves no room for discussion or argument. In both cases, individual and social life is regulated in a totalitarian fashion that does not tolerate any democratic discussion or difference of views. Followers see their own religion or racial group as innately superior to others. Radicals among them feel they have a divine mission to impose their religion on all others. In doing so, they find the recourse to violence and terror justified by the sacred mission with which they are entrusted.

The growth of these movements leads obviously to conflict and confrontation within the same society, as well as internationally. It also creates a fertile ground for autocratic rule and the outbreak of conflicts.[11] The growth of such tendencies has paradoxically occurred at a time when the influence of human rights groups is at its apex. It is as if there is dialectical alternation between nationalism and internationalism or a struggle between the desire to impose a racial or religious totalitarian rule, on the one hand, and the yearning for the liberation of man based on the universality of the values of human dignity, freedom and well-being.

Human Rights, from Protection to Exploitation

The human rights movement, in its current organized form, rose from the ashes of Nazism and fascism.

The idea of protecting the rights of man within his own country matured by the end of World War II. The 1944 San Francisco Conference did show that the promotion of the values and institutions of democracy and justice are needed to ensure the prevention of wars and the protection of the international community from extremist regimes and hostile thought. Such objectives also require respect for basic human rights as a means to prevent the emergence of totalitarian currents, which upon seizing power impose non-democratic regimes which ban any opposition and incite fanaticism and hatred of others.

The United Nations Charter establishes a connection between domestic and international peace. It establishes also a link between the security of the international community and its capacity to protect man and safeguard his freedom and dignity at home within a free and democratic society which guarantees his development and well-being. The spirit of the Charter in 1945 was more comprehensive than that of today's world order. The national leaders assembled at that time felt that no true security could be established without ensuring the welfare of all humanity, reducing the gap between peoples and establishing goodwill, solidarity and coexistence between all nations.

Man has always struggled for freedom and dignity. But such a struggle took an organized and institutional shape with the creation of the United Nations. The concept of universality of human rights that was gradually consecrated within the United Nations and its specialized agencies is the same concept that prevails today. This universal vision gained the upper hand over the idea of the specificity of human rights and relativity to culture, civilization and religion. In his speeches, President Ben Ali has stressed the universality of human rights, differentiating between the values which are held in common by all mankind and the means of their implementation, which differ according to the circumstances of the various societies and their capacity of stability and growth.[12]

The United Nations and its agencies have consistently endeavored to free man from the control of the state, and to confirm the UN's mandate as overseer of the rights of man, and as guarantor of his freedoms vis-à-vis others in general, and the state in particular. Toward this end, they sought the assistance of a large network of non-governmental organizations, both national and transnational. These organizations were relied upon as consultants, but the relationship grew in complexity and it became increasingly difficult to determine who is influencing whom, and who is the actual decision-maker. The number of human rights organizations and the people involved in their activities grew so much that these institutions acquired the characteristics of a real bureaucracy, and became a huge, bulky apparatus whose course and objectives are not always easy to fathom or predict.

This was the origin of paradoxical situations on the international human rights scene. I have been myself privy to events when it was not clear anymore

6

whether this huge human rights apparatus still had its eyes on the objectives toward which it was created.

There was undoubtedly an irony in the fact that extremist and fanatical groups were able to receive the support of human rights organizations and take advantage of the clout of such organizations.[13] Under various pretenses, such as the respect for difference of opinion, for freedom of religion and for the rights of minorities, fanatical groups have succeeded in winning the active support of non-governmental human rights organizations. The latter made their lobbying, decision-making and public outreach mechanisms in Europe and the United States available to extremist groups. These groups in turn offered human rights groups ample ammunition for interference and high profile intervention. This led human rights groups to fall in a large trap, without serving the cause of human rights.[14]

History shows how fanaticism and radicalism can grow and blossom in a climate of democracy if no effort is made to pre-empt its growth and cut off its supply lines. It shows how since the early 1980s human rights groups, which were created to fight fanaticism, became unwittingly the protector of just such movements.

Claiming to be human rights victims, fundamentalist movements were able to influence democratic public opinion. As in the Nazi and Fascist eras, fundamentalists are trying to take advantage of democracy to seize control of power and establish a totalitarian system that will first and foremost do away with democracy and human rights. The best illustration of this danger is the situation in fundamentalist-ruled countries.

In 1991, President Ben Ali entrusted me with the task of contacting certain human rights NGOs, including Amnesty International. The objective was to draw the attention of these organizations to the dangers inherent in defending fanatical groups which preach hatred and are involved in violence. Initially, Amnesty International did not alter its policy of support to extremist groups. It arrived at a different understanding of the issues only after subsequent contacts. It announced a different position in 1992 when it was confronted with the events in Algeria, which produced a large number of casualties and demonstrated without the shadow of a doubt the violent radicalism of fundamentalists. The first formal denunciation of violence by non-governmental groups was issued by Amnesty in view of the events in Algeria. Since that time, it has denounced the actions of both governmental and non-governmental groups.

The position advocated by Tunisia in its contacts with Amnesty International and similar other groups is that the real danger to human rights is the propagation of fanatical thought, and that the main source of abuses is extremist groups and not governments.[15] The danger does not emanate from the reaction to extremist thought but from the dissemination and promotion of this thought. Abuses, which may be committed by police officers, could be denounced and punished. But it is rather difficult to oppose hate thought and totalitarian ideologies.

Always in Tunisia, we have shared the point of view that uncovering the practices of governments serves the cause of human rights. We have also recognized the intervention of governments and NGOs within or outside the United Nations as unarguably acceptable. This has been often reiterated by President Ben Ali. We have also believed that human rights mechanisms are in need of more fine tuning, so as not to lose sight of their mission. Such mechanisms should not become a liability for humanity by unsuspectingly offering aid and support to fanatical thought and its violent forms of expression. That would constitute an added threat to societies and cause more tensions on the international scene.

Added to this deviation in the course of human rights activism is the double-standard policy adopted on more than one occasion, as well as the obvious influence of superpowers in United Nations decision making, and the role played by certain human rights groups in conflicts such as in Bosnia, Chechnya, Rwanda and Burundi. Other questions arise concerning the treatment of human rights situations in certain Middle East countries. All such considerations can only muddy up the view of the human rights scene and raise questions about the political ulterior motives behind positions that are normally taken on purely humanitarian grounds.[16]

Extremists have found a haven in traditional democracies, where they particularly took advantage of democratic freedoms. They have received political asylum there, although they have previously committed crimes, and in some cases acts of terrorism, in their countries of origin. Some, who had been involved in issuing orders for assassination and bomb attacks, today enjoy the status of political refugees. They are allowed total freedom of action by their host countries, who are normally under obligation not to allow them to engage in acts which are hostile to their countries of origin. This has had an inhibitive effect on the mechanisms of judicial cooperation. Despite the seriousness of their crimes, which have nothing to do with crimes of opinion, they have enjoyed refugee status. Almost publicly, they engage in arms trafficking, falsification of documents and other acts which are not part of any usual peaceful political activities. Tunisia did in fact provide evidence that some of them have applied for political asylum using false documents and that they have continued their involvement in terrorist activities. It is only today that Europe has started to feel the danger of those it chose to harbor as refugees, some of the latter having been implicated in acts of terror in Europe itself.

Any practitioner of politics will notice that fundamentalists have, since the 1980s, enjoyed the protection of human rights organizations. To a certain extent, this has continued up to the present, posing an additional obstacle in the road to pluralism. This was quite intriguing for the leaders of certain countries, who expected encouragement for their efforts in democracy building and in fighting against fanatical movements, but found themselves instead the target of harassment and denigration. This paradoxical situation has had practical implications, as certain industrial powers and international financial institutions have established a linkage between the respect for human rights and the allocation of loans and investment credits. This premise is quite problematic, considering that emerging democracies need economic support more than others, in order

8

to reduce the pockets of poverty and unemployment and contain the socio-economic pressures which are the main breeding grounds of extremism.

The best example that comes to mind is that of Algeria, where the government has been trying to build a democracy that is free of extremism. It has confronted extremists who called upon foreign governments and international financial institutions to suspend all support to Algeria. They hoped by that to make the domestic crisis there even worse, and by doing so increase the appeal of extremism and therefore the likelihood of a fundamentalist takeover. For a brief period of time, Tunisia faced the same opposition. Leaders and *sponsors* of the fundamentalist movement *Nahdha,* who are close to figures from the Gulf region, tried to use whatever influence they had to deprive Tunisia of foreign assistance and the support of regional financial institutions.

These issues were among the questions discussed with Western democratic figures, whether parliamentarians, academics, media people or human rights activists. Our reproach to them was that they lacked deep knowledge of fundamentalism, that they often took fundamentalist rhetoric at face value[17] and that they looked at democratization through a Western prism that did not take into consideration the complexity of the democratic process and the special situation of each society in this regard.

No One Way

The path followed by Tunisia toward democratization was different from that of other societies. There was never one single way, or a single pace, to democracy. The road leading there was never strewn with the same type of obstacles.

Certain governments did not know how to spare their countries a painful transition to democracy. Instead of a smooth process, they had to go through a bumpy and arduous journey. As the first stage of French democracy, the French Revolution created heavy casualties. It unleashed a long period of chaos and strife before a final equilibrium ensuring justice and freedom could be reached. The same was true for Germany, Italy and Spain. The one possible exception was Britain, where the process was relatively gradual and incremental and therefore the human toll of the democratic process was not as heavy.

More recently, the struggle for democracy during the last decade had been quite dramatic. In many instances, government leaders could not steer the ship of state on the right course during the particularly sensitive early stages of the transition to political pluralism.[18]

One example is that of Mikhail Gorbachev, who because of lack of the proper political infrastructure and institutions caused the dislocation of the Soviet Union as a superpower and implosion of its society. Without establishing the proper instruments or preparing the necessary dialogue for such a change, he pushed his country precipitately. He was overtaken by events and the pent-up frustrations of seven decades of dictatorial rule led to an explosion of the aspirations to liberation and independence. Power shifted toward the opposition. The new system that took over was ostensibly pluralistic. But it was in reality precarious in nature and still needed many years of maturation before reaching a reasonable balance allowing for a healthy form of competition. Gorbachev realized what he had wrought only after he lost power. Then he learned in hindsight that he should have prepared the ground for political transition by establishing the bases of a free-market economy, offsetting the social impact of the dismantling of the state economy and appeasing the nationalistic tendencies which transformed the previous relations of cooperation between republics into hostility and open confrontation.

Gorbachev should have provided for a harmonious *modus vivendi* between the various nationalities and ethnic and religious groups. That would have prevented the new degree of liberty and democracy from serving only as a catalyst for the break-up of the Soviet Union, and the dismantling of a large social space, which used to represent a more adequate framework for economic development and a more efficient means of international participation. Among other things, Gorbachev did not take his time to mold a new discourse, establish new pluralistic institutions and create a new political culture. He could not reconcile the demands of his party with the pressures for independence. Until 1987, *Perestroika* remained at the level of discourse. In a speech before the top brass of the Communist Party and the State, he explained on December 3, 1984, that *Perestroika* constituted the "biggest challenge" and that he hoped to reinforce "the capacity of the Soviet Union to enter the new millennium as a prosperous superpower."[19]

Gorbachev did not lay the ground for such a policy and did not, as analysts later pointed out, "set aside the necessary timeframe" for it. "As soon as democracy was established, nationalist tendencies emerged on the political scene and swept everything in their way."[20] In January, 1987, he wondered out loud about the "guarantees" which would ensure the success of the reform movement.

The press was suddenly free of all inhibitions. It started to investigate all the previously concealed layers of society and unleash a 70-year backlog of anger and frustration.

Gorbachev could not change the structures of his party in a manner that would have allowed him to implement his policies. At the grassroot elections of June 21, 1987, no change took place. This compelled Gorbachev to look for support outside the party. Ben Ali avoided making the same mistake after the leadership transition of 1987. It was suggested then that he create a new party other than the Democratic Constitutional Rally (RCD) or spread a network of "November 7 Clubs" as rival structures to the RCD, but he did not. Gorbachev chose on the contrary to mobilize his supporters for the creation of "popular fronts" that would prod civil society to better participate in *Perestroika*. This approach alarmed the party leadership while it encouraged nationalist trends.

Other currents were trying to accelerate the pace of change. They were led by Boris Yeltsin, a man with a large following because of his appeal to the many who were yearning for a better future. He unexpectedly received 89.6% of the votes in Moscow. This encouraged him to enter the national race and help build a coalition between nationalist trends and the pro-democracy movement.

As explained by Jean Elleinstein,[21] the winds of democracy in the Soviet Union swept away everything, including the Union of Soviet Republics and Gorbachev himself.[22] The writer Aitamatov introduced Gorbachev's bid for the presidency by describing him as the "man who awakened the kingdom from its sleep. He should, however, admit the mistakes he made at the start of *Perestroika,* in the economic field and in the relations between nationalities." He was quickly overtaken by events. The insubordination of the Army and intelligence services became obvious. The state apparatus became dysfunctional. The Communist Party lost its position. The May 1, 1990 celebrations turned into anti-Gorbachev demonstrations, forcing the latter from the viewing stage. Even NATO became preoccupied with the turn of events. Gradually, positions within the Communist Party hardened and support for the conservative wing within the party widened, to the detriment of Gorbachev. On May 29, 1990, Yeltsin was elected President of the Russian Federation. He took advantage of the political vacuum in the State and the Party to consolidate his hold on power. But the Soviet Union was but a shadow of what it once used to be. Nationalist movements gained momentum and internecine strife intensified. The economy weakened while trafficking and other criminal activities became widespread. Instead of entering the next millennium as a "prosperous superpower," as Gorbachev hoped, the former Soviet Union has become, on the eve of the new century, a foreign aid recipient and a nation with only limited freedom of decision.

The second example is that of former president Chedly Benjedid of Algeria. His policies cost Algeria dearly in the course of democratization. Algeria started on the path of democratization right after Tunisia, but it chose a different course. In the face of the great upheaval of October, 1988, it opened the floodgates of pluralism without adequate examination of the possible repercussions of its decisions regarding the creation of political parties and electoral representation. In less than a month, more than 60 parties were formed. It was predictable that the parties with the largest following in this period of transition would be those which would appeal to the yearning for identity, or advocate rapid and radical change. It was therefore the most extremist of all parties, the Islamic Salvation Front (FIS), which earned more dividends than others. The Berber movement was also among the beneficiaries. New splinter parties emerged while the former ruling party, the National Liberation Front (FLN), failed to carry out any introspection. No real attempts at self-criticism or readjustment were made.

Algeria entered a period of chaos. Premature municipal elections led to the victory of hard-line fundamentalists. Out of the control of the municipal councils, the latter were able to influence the course of the subsequent legislative elections and win the first round.[23] In a meeting with Algerian President Benjedid, then-Tunisian Minister of the Interior Abdallah Kallel explained to his Algerian interlocutor the main elements of the Tunisian approach. Kallel stressed the dangers inherent in opening the way to fundamentalists and made the point that fundamentalists could, in Algeria's delicate transition period, gain more votes than were representative of their real size. Benjedid replied with a harsh tone that each country is entitled to its own approach, and said that only the results will show which course is better. He added that within one year he would lead his country to a full-fledged democracy. Instead, and within a few months of this meeting, on January 11, 1992, Benjedid was removed from power and asked to resign. The army seized power and installed a Higher State Council. Mohamed Boudhiaf was asked to serve as the President of the Council. Boudhiaf corrected the course and suspended the elections. He proceeded on a gradual and prudent policy and endeavored to establish the institutional bases of democracy in Algeria. He had, however, closed the door which was previously opened by others. Fundamentalists and other political contenders had won a number of positions and had thought their victory near. Boudhiaf found himself at an impasse. After only a few months in office, on June 29, 1992, Boudhiaf was killed. He was replaced by Ali Kefi, who followed the same course. Since July 10, 1993, President Liamine Zeroual has assumed the task of leadership with great clarity of purpose and a high level of achievement.[24] But Algeria never deserved the losses it incurred. These included about 40.000 dead from both sides, a continuous expenditure of economic resources and the failed process of democratization that did not proceed with cautious gradualism.

Both Soviet and Algerian examples show very well how difficult the transition period can be. They also demonstrate the need for caution in establishing pluralism and the necessity of gradualism in filling the political vacuum left by the previous one-party system. Any shift from one extreme to the other can only lead to socially-onerous deviations and delay if not indefinitely postpone the advent of pluralism. Opening the floodgates can unleash a devastating flood with no sense of direction.[25]

There is no one way to pluralism. All the countries of Eastern Europe, with their varying degrees of success in doing away with the one-party system, are one case in point. In all cases, however, the transition to pluralism has proven to be less costly in countries where transitions were handled with caution and where the emergence of extremist and nationalist currents was prevented, at least for a limited period of time. The likelihood of success was also enhanced in countries where proper care was taken to lay the ground socially and economically for pluralism, and where individuals and institutions were adequately prepared for the culture of competition and for the free market of ideas. In this regard, it is our belief that Tunisia was quite successful.

The Dynamic of Democracy

Various definitions have been offered for democracy. A quite simple and clear definition is offered here. Democracy is meant as the form of government which allows people to exercise power directly or indirectly through their chosen representatives. Democracy is not, however, meant to be a static situation but a dynamic process.[26] Popular participation may be wider in one democratic system than in another. It could more obvious at one stage of social development than in another.

Democratic systems provide for the suspension under certain conditions of institutional rule during the times of crises. Democracies make provisions for the establishment of states of emergency when security, stability and at times the survival of the state itself are at stake. Without stability and the ability of the state to impose the rule of law, society crumbles and democracy is replaced by chaos and anarchy.

The degree of participation in public life varies from one democracy to the other.[27] All systems, however, are considered democratic that guarantee the rights of citizens to vote and to present their candidacies in regular elections, and allow the free expression of opposite views in public fora.

There are old democracies with time-honored traditions, such as the systems in place in Western Europe and North America. And there are also nascent democracies, such as those in certain countries of the Mediterranean, in Eastern Europe, in the former Soviet Union and Africa. Such democracies can be ranked according to different criteria, such as the state of freedoms, the respect of opposing views, the frequency and credibility of elections, the decision-making influence of pressure groups, the degree of monopoly of the means to influence elections and public opinions.[28]

According to Jacques Rupnick, political transition in central Eastern Europe requires a form of "democratic renewal."[29] He also thinks that all political definitions—including that of pluralism—need to be redefined. He believes as well that the first elections in emerging democracies are *constitutive* elections."[30] Schmitter and O'Donnell explain that in traditional democracies electoral competition is between structured forces and about agreed-upon legitimacy. In emerging democracies, the function of elections is to establish such a framework. According to the model suggested by Benjamin Constant, the stake in emerging democracies is less in actual participation than in enjoying the freedom to do so. The danger in this type of system, he adds, is that democracy becomes an elite struggle without any roots in society. He also believes that the danger of a return to a one-party system and authoritarianism remains a possibility as long as the economy does not take off and the bases of the newly-created institutions are not solidified.

The real political practice within different democracies is not always what it is believed to be or what it should be ideally. There are degrees of imperfection and in the concealment of the imperfections of political practice. Aside from the imbalances which are considered to be legitimate, such as the uneven control of the media, traditional democracies are occasionally shaken by political scandal regarding the illegal financing of political campaigns, eavesdropping on rival parties, taking advantage of public trust or public funds for political gain, and using the judiciary to harm opponents.

It is therefore difficult to claim that there is one system or one standard for democracy. Those who criticize the flaws in the democratic system of another country often miss more serious shortcomings in their own system of government. Emerging democracies should not be embarrassed by their shortcomings, nor should they hesitate to control the instruments of democracy and to impose whatever temporary restrictions may be required, providing such restrictions are needed in the transition period and will lead to a free and democratic society. They should not be affected by the criticisms of certain Western analysts who are condescending in their views of the developing world and are quite dismissive of the developing countries' democratization efforts. They use as a sole yardstick the situation in Western democracies and do not take into consideration the dynamic nature of democracy in relation with the situation in every society.

It is to be pointed out here that the point of view of political practitioners is more realistic and appreciates the difficulty of the transition from one-party-rule to pluralism.

The United Nations Organization has itself recognized the individual character of democracy. This is made clear in the Covenant on Political and Civil Rights adopted in 1966. In all human rights agreements there are clauses which enable governments to restrict or temporarily suspend rights and freedoms when necessary, as long as the objective is the building of a free democratic society. Exempted from such possible restriction are the natural inalienable rights such as the freedom of expression and faith, the right to physical integrity, and the interdiction of torture, exile and slavery.   .

From this vantage point one can understand Ben Ali's approach to democratization, which takes into consideration certain necessary balances and follows a well-established gradualist process. The same approach provides for a comprehensive simultaneous action on several tracks as a prelude to the establishment of democracy. Action was taken on several fronts at the same time, always taking into consideration the need to safeguard the spirit of national consensus and ensure the stability without which no political system can endure or achieve its priorities with the least cost and in the shortest time possible.

Many political analysts have highlighted the specificities of the Tunisian approach and attempted to explain the country's two-fold success in achieving development and ensuring stability, focusing on the strategy of comprehensive action and the various repercussions of the liberal transition.

Tunisia used security and legal means to thwart fundamentalism, adopting a comprehensive approach which consisted in eradicating pockets of poverty, creating jobs for young people, imbuing children with new values, and freeing economic initiative to make development more than just a precarious structure upheld only by the efforts of the State. Furthermore, incentives have been provided to increase public awareness of the importance of hard work and progress, and to mobilize people within political parties, associations and various institutions of civil society, to ensure that the action against fundamentalism is based upon an effort that is commonly shared and complete. In this way, Tunisia has succeeded in transforming the State's struggle against extremism into a fight led by the entire society, and this in turn had dried up all the potential breeding grounds for fundamentalism.

If one looks closely at the laws and decrees that have been passed, and at the effort of mobilization and information that has accompanied them, one can perceive the consistency of the approach.

It is clear, and should not be overlooked, that Ben Ali's method is one of strategic progression in the implementation of these actions, a progression which advances simultaneously on three fronts.

The first front is that of response to the plethora of demands released by the change in leadership that took place on November 7, 1987. The population's ambitions were all the stronger in that the change was long overdue, and the entire country now placed the greatest hope in its new leader. At the same time, the ambitions of extremist movements—relieved from suffocation—were not long in becoming apparent, and they began attempting to exploit the Change to their own advantage and to channel pent-up anger to the accomplishment of their objectives. The new regime had to streamline these tendencies.

The second front consisted in the restructuring of authority. Following many years of decline, it was necessary to correct the orientation of the State and to rebuild the party in power, which called for a long, hard effort and for prudent and cautious action to avoid alienating supporters. The interest in revitalizing the capacities of the single party and preparing it to adjust to a multi-party system most clearly marks Ben Ali's method and sets it apart from so many other approaches, notably in the Soviet Union and in Algeria.

The third front, undoubtedly the broadest and most difficult, is that which aims at the building of a democratic opposition. Not all observers, perhaps, are aware that Ben Ali's prime concern was to establish a new climate that would favor a strong, healthy opposition, and he continues consistently to strengthen this so as to fill the gap left by the old, one-party system.

It is my conviction that Ben Ali's most characteristic feature is his profound conviction that the Change will not be complete so long as it has not prepared the way for active democratic opposition, an opposition capable of competing with the party in power, mobilizing the various sectors of civil society, and influencing public opinion. *This alone will make it possible to set up the conditions that will enable the democratic system to run effectively. There is nothing to be feared in seeing the doors open wide, so long as extremism finds no vacuum to fill, no troubled waters in which to fish. It will be reduced to its real dimension, which must, in a democratic system, be marginal and secondary.*

Something of which foreign observers are unaware is that building a sound opposition, subscribing to the common values of the entire society, is the most difficult task an emerging democracy can face. It is not a countermove, nor a superficial construction, but a real effort of self-development. It cannot be accomplished by the regime itself, for in that case it could not be an independent opposition. It must, on the other hand, be given a favorable climate and tools with which to unify its forces, publicize its programs, and mobilize followers around it, so that it can compete with other parties and convince public opinion that it is a valid alternative. □

THE FIRST CHALLENGE:
Controlling the Outflow

Change...and the Utilization of Change

SATURDAY, NOVEMBER 7, 1987, was no ordinary day. The news it brought was totally unexpected. That day, at 6:30 a.m., Tunisians woke up to a solemn, determined voice reading the following statement:

> "In the name of God, the Clement, the Merciful.
>
> Fellow citizens,
>
> We, Zine El Abidine Ben Ali, Prime Minister of the Republic of Tunisia, proclaim the following:
>
> The great sacrifices made by the leader Habīb Bourguiba, first president of the Republic of Tunisia, together with other men of valor, for the liberation and development of Tunisia, are countless. And that is why we granted him our affection and regard and worked under his leadership for many years confidently, faithfully and in a spirit of self-denial, at all levels, in the ranks of our popular and national army and in the government. But the onset of his senility and the deterioration of his health, and the medical report made on this, called us to carry out our national duty and declare him totally incapable of undertaking the tasks of President of the Republic. Thereby, acting under Article 57 of the Constitution, with the help of God, we take up the Presidency of the Republic and the high command of our armed forces.
>
> In the exercise of our responsibilities, we are counting on all the children of our dear country to work together in an atmosphere of confidence, security and serenity, from which all hatred and rancor will be banished.

17

The independence of our country, our territorial integrity, the invulnerability of our fatherland and our people's progress are a matter of concern for all citizens. Love of one's country, devotion to its safety, commitment to its growth are the sacred duties of all Tunisians.

Fellow citizens,

Our people has reached a degree of responsibility and maturity where every individual and group is in a position to constructively contribute to the running of its affairs, in conformity with the republican idea which gives institutions their full scope and guarantees the conditions for a responsible democracy, fully respecting the sovereignty of the people as written into the Constitution. This Constitution needs urgent revision. The times in which we live can no longer admit of life presidency or automatic succession, from which the people is excluded. Our people deserves an advanced and institutionalized political life, truly based on the plurality of parties and mass organizations.

We shall be soon putting forward a bill that will concern political parties and another concerning the press, which ensure a wider participation in the building up of Tunisia and the strengthening of her independence in a context of order and discipline.

We shall see that the law is correctly enforced in a way that will proscribe any kind of iniquity or injustice. We shall act to restore the prestige of the State and to put an end to chaos and laxity. There will be no more favoritism or indifference where the squandering of the country's wealth is concerned.

We shall continue to keep up our good relations and positive cooperation with all other countries, particularly friendly and sister countries. We shall respect our international engagements.

We shall give Islamic, Arab, African and Mediterranean solidarity its due importance. We shall strive ourselves to achieve the unity, based on our common interests, of the Great Maghreb.

Fellow citizens,

By the Grace of God, we are entering on a new era of efforts and determination.

Love of our country and the call of duty require this of us.
Long live Tunisia!
Long live the Republic!"

بيان ٧ نوفمبر ١٩٨٧

بسم الله الرحمن الرحيم

نحن زين العابدين بن علي الوزير الأول بمعهد الرئيسة أصدرنا البلاغ التالي

أيتها المواطنات أيها المواطنون

إن التضحيات الجسام التي قُدم عليها ـ

رمقة رجال بررة ـ الزعيم الحبيب بورقيبة ـ

أول رئيس للجمهورية التونسية بي سبيل

تحرير تونس وتنميتها ـ لا تحصى ولا تعد ،

لذلك أحببناه وقدرناه وعملنا السنين

الطوال تحت امرته بي مختلف المستويات

بي جيشنا الوطني الشعبي وبي الحكومة

بثقة وإخلاص وتبان ـ

ولكن الواجب الوطني يفرض علينا اليوم

أمام طول شيخوخته واستعجال موته أن نعلن

اعتمادنا على تقرير طبي

أنه أصبح عاجزا تماما على الإطلاع بمهامه

كرئيس للجمهورية وقد جاء ليؤكد هذا

نيابة

19

تقرير طبي أمضاه . . . .

وبناءً على ذلك وعملاً بالعمل 57 من

الدستور أتولّى بعون الله

وتوفيقه رئاسة الجمهورية والقيادة

العليا لقواتنا المسلحة .

وسأعتمد في مباشرة مسؤولياتنا

في جو من الثقة والأمن والاطمئنان

على كل أبناء تونسنا العزيزة ، ولا مكان

للحقد والبغضاء والكراهية .

إن استقلال بلادنا وسلامة ترابنا ومناعة

وطننا وتقدم شعبنا هي مسؤولية كلّ

تونسي بدون تمييز، التونسيّ

وحبّ الوطن والذود عنه والرفع
من شأنه واجب مقدس على كل مواطن
أيها المواطنون أيتها المواطنات
إن شعبنا بلغ من الوعي والنضج ما يسمح
لكل أبنائه وبناته بالمشاركة البناءة
في تصريف شؤونه، في ظل نظام جمهوري
يولي المؤسسات حق قدرها ويوفر
أسباب الديمقراطية المسؤولة، وعلى
أساس سيادة الشعب كما نص عليها
الدستور الذي يحتاج إلى مراجعة أصبحت
اليوم مؤكدة. ولا مجال اليوم في عصرنا
إلى رئاسة مدى الحياة وإلى الخلافة آلية
لا دخل فيها للشعب.

21

إن شعبنا جدير بحياة سياسية
متطورة متقدمة ومنظمة ، تعتمد بحق
تعددية الأحزاب السياسية
والتنظيمات الشعبية .
وإننا سنعرض قريبا مشروع قانون
للأحزاب ومشروع قانون للصحافة
يوفران مساهمة أوسع بنظام ومسؤولية
في بناء تونس ودعم استقلالها ،
وسأحرص على إعطاء القانون حرمته ، ولا
مجال للظلم و القهر وسأحرص على إعطاء الدولة
هيبتها ، ولا مكان للمحسوبية والتسيب
ولا سبيل لاستغلال النفوذ أو التساهل
في أموال المجموعة ومكاسبها .

22

وسنأخا فظ على حسن علاقاتنا
وتعاوننا مع كل الدول وأخص بالذكر
منها الدول الشقيقة والصديقة مع   لا سيما
التأكيد على احترام تعهداتنا   كما نعلن
والتزاماتنا الدولية وسنحطى
المرتبة
لتفا مننا الإسلامي والعربي
والإفريقي والمتوسطي المكانة التي
بستحقها ء وسنعمل بخطى ثابتة وهي
نطاق المصلحة المشتركة على تجسيم
المستقى
نطاق المصلحة
وحدة المغرب العربي الكبير
أيتها المواطنات (أيها المواطنون)
إنه عهد جديد نبنيه مع بعضنا بعض
معا على بركة الله جلّ وعزّم، وهو

23

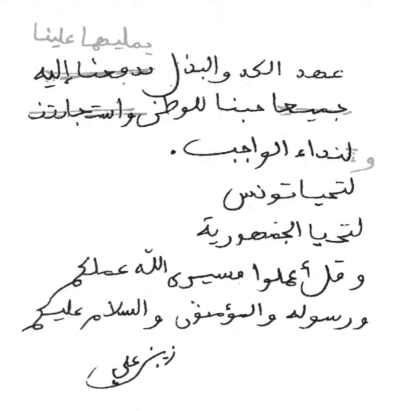

عهد الكد والبذل تعهدنا الله يمليها علينا
جميعا حبنا للوطن واستجابت
و لنداء الواجب .
لتحيا تونس
لتحيا الجمهورية
و قل اعملوا مسيرى الله عليكم
ورسوله والمؤمنون و السلام عليكم
زين بن علي

24

The population, suddenly relieved, quickly propagated the news, taking to the streets in great numbers from all ages and walks of life to salute the man who undertook the change which literally saved the nation and renewed hope and confidence in the future. Tunisians did not know then that the effect of salvation was double: not only the man who grew old over an exhausted and diminished regime, but also the nation were saved from an imminent *coup d'état* by fundamentalists scheduled for Sunday morning, November 8.

The event which Tunisians had anticipated for years finally occurred, and it occurred in a civilized manner unknown previously in the region. Ben Ali acted under Article 57 of the Constitution, which provides for a transfer of power to the Prime Minister should the President of the Republic be confirmed to have become permanently unfit for the tasks of the presidency. There was no bloodshed, and no retribution against former officials. On the contrary, honor and gratitude were expressed to the leader Bourguiba and all Tunisian patriots. The Change was immaculate, without injury or resentment. It was an act of building without demolition, an addition without diminution.

At this point, we must introduce the man who undertook the Change. Zine El Abidine Ben Ali was born on September 3, 1936 in Hammam-Sousse, a small town in the Tunisian Sahel. From the modest environment in which he grew up, he inherited a propensity for the virtues of simplicity, discretion and generosity. He embraced political militancy while still in high school in Sousse, serving as liaison between the Neo-Destour Party, the party currently in power, and the militants involved in armed struggle against French colonialism. This activism cost him imprisonment and exclusion from all schools in Tunisia. He resumed his studies after some time and persevered into higher education. In appreciation of his abilities, the Party sent him to France as one of a group destined to form the nucleus of the future national army. He pursued his training at the distinguished Inter-Arms School of Saint-Cyr, from which he graduated. He subsequently earned several diplomas from other equally prestigious institutions such as the Artillery School at Châlons-Sur-Marne in France, the Senior Intelligence School and the School of Anti-Aircraft Field Artillery in the United States. He was still a young officer when he was called on in 1964 to set up the Military Security Department, which he ran for ten years. In 1974 he was appointed Military Attaché in Morocco and Spain and spent three years in Rabat. In 1977, he was entrusted with the Director-Generalship of National Security where he demonstrated special skills in organization and follow-up. In April 1980 he was appointed Ambassador to Warsaw, Poland, where for four years he mastered the art of diplomacy. In 1984, he was called back as the head of National Security, and within a few months, on October 29, 1984, was appointed Secretary of State in charge of National Security.

Bourguiba came to appreciate the ability, skills and distinctive patriotism of Ben Ali. He also came to realize that Ben Ali was the man he could depend on to save the regime from an explosive social and political pressure. As events quickly unfolded, Ben Ali's responsibilities increased. Within one year, on October 23, 1985, Bourguiba appointed him Minister in charge of National Security, and a few months later, on April 28, 1986, Minister of the Interior. In June of the same year, Ben Ali became a Member of the Political Bureau of the Party where the major decisions are taken, and was soon appointed Assistant Secretary General of the Party. Promoted to the rank of Minister of State on May 16, 1987, he remained in charge of the Interior. On October 2, 1987, he was appointed Prime Minister while keeping the Interior portfolio. He was then 51 years old. At the same time, he became Secretary-General of the Destourian Socialist Party. Ben Ali had a reputation for discipline, efficiency and discretion. He kept at once aloof from and above the intrigues and rivalries of the seraglio, sought instead to establish dialogue with such political forces as the trade unions and the Tunisian Human Rights League, and advised President Bourguiba with a realistic policy to reconnect with society. But when he realized that the edifice threatened to crumble under the President's advanced age and his inability to face responsibility, and that the leadership and the regime were in hopeless crisis, he took his bold initiative within constitutional bounds and with a distinctively civilized style.

The Declaration expressed what most Tunisians felt at that time. They had respect for Habib Bourguiba as one of the leaders of the liberation movement, and recognized his distinguished service to the country. However, his advanced age coupled with his failing health since the end of the 1960s made him vulnerable to the maneuvers of courtesans. He was no longer in touch with reality and ought to have stepped down. But his self-proclamation as President for Life in 1974 had transformed the power struggle into a struggle for succession, thus jeopardizing the survival of the whole regime.[31]

By the end of the 1960s anger had built up among all groups of society, and the political leadership sank into isolation and a monopoly of power. Criticism grew into pent-up frustration. And except for a few crises, such as the trade union uprising of 1978 and the bread riots of 1984 which served as temporary escape valves, social frustration persisted in the absence of any means of expression. The 1987 Change created high aspirations among Tunisians and at the same time brought intense pressure to bear upon the new regime. Using the terms of modern political analysis, one could say that the input began to outweigh the output, and that the capacity to meet demand and to control social and economic factors must be especially strong and effective, so that the new regime might absorb and channel the outflow according to the new priorities.[32]

The Change provoked, in large sectors of the national elite, a desire to participate in the exercise of power and in the decision-making process after so many years of exclusion. It also created a general desire to lift restrictions and establish freedom after a long period of frustration, a strong desire for equality before the law, for the establishment of justice without discrimination, and for the elimination of all forms of despotism and oppression. It also created a yearning to reconfirm the nation's Arab-Islamic identity after years of marginalization and undiscerning allegiance to foreign values, to limit the encroachments of bureaucracy, and alleviate the burden of administrative regulations and promote private initiative. The Change also created a desire to prevent the mismanagement of public funds and punish corruption, and to safeguard public property. These and a host of other aspirations, which the new regime had to control and channel, emerged concurrently.

At the same time, hostile movements which were underground during Bourguiba's reign emerged to take advantage of the Change. They were pre-empted by Ben Ali who moved quickly to assume control effectively. Those movements were frustrated to lose the leadership, or to use their own terms, frustrated not to reap the fruit which they thought they had cultivated. What the fundamentalist movements wanted was not to "rectify or reform" society but to "revolutionize it radically from top to bottom," to grab power and use the state apparatus for their own benefit. Such were the terms used at that time by the leaders of the so-called Movement of the Islamic Tendency, Salah Karkar and Rached Ghannouchi.[33]

The November 7th Change caught the latter Movement by surprise, and the vast popular support for President Ben Ali cooled its will to act. The fundamentalist leaders pretended to go along with the Change and voiced support for the new president, banking on the forthcoming elections to step forth and win a majority vote, or at least appear, before public opinion, as the real alternative to the party in power. This was for them a strategic step on the way to taking over and establishing an "Islamic" state. However, the legislative elections of April 2, 1989, in which they participated on independent lists and for which they deployed all their energy, demonstrated the limit of their size, with a meager 8% of the vote. Political observers were aware that those votes were inflated, that the use of independent lists enabled them to gain wider sympathy, and that most of the 13.6% won by the independent lists, which included the fundamentalists and the Communist Workers Party, went less *for* them than *against* the regime. Failing to exploit the change through elections, the fundamentalists realized that the democratic procedure was not the quick passport to power which they had thought it would be. In the aftermath of the elections, their leader Rached Ghannouchi chose to go into voluntary exile and left the country on May 28, 1989. Commenting on his choice, some observers said that Ghannouchi admired the Iranian revolution to the extent that he tried to imitate Khomeini and envisioned a triumphant return at the head of a total revolution. Except that, as Dunn puts it, "Tunisia is not Iran, and while Bourguiba had some faults in common with the Shah, Ben Ali is not Bourguiba."[34] Some members of the Islamic Tendency have spoken of a deep conflict then between Ghannouchi and the number-two man in the Movement, Abdelfattah Mourou. Subsequent events have demonstrated that Ghannouchi wanted to leave after setting up a secret branch which he entrusted Mohamed Chammam to run under his personal orders, and devising options to "take" power—which in the Movement's parlance is a euphemism for power grabbing. Abroad, Ghannouchi wavered between support for terrorist operations which he delegated his partisans to undertake, and denial—depending on the spirit of public opinion and the morale of his partisans. This wavering increased his isolation within his movement and his loss of credibility outside it.

We must pause for awhile and explain how the so-called *Nahdha* Movement came about, so that the reader may understand its ideological roots, the origin of its organization, the growth of its secret branch, and the influence on it of other "fundamentalist" movements. It is necessary to focus on the "fundamentalists" in this chapter because they were the real obstacle to a nascent democracy. With them there will be no democracy. And without civil opposition, it will be difficult for democracy to take root. The political system will therefore have to make a special effort to break the fundamentalist network and prepare the ground for the other opposition, the healthy one.

Ghannouchi played an important role in this association after returning from Syria in 1969. In 1973 *Al Maarifa* magazine was created by this association, which managed in 1978 to take control of *Al Mujtamaa* magazine and *Al Habib* newspaper. The content of these publications became increasingly political, focusing on the practical means of establishing an "Islamic state."

The Fundamentalist Threat: Two Faces and a Dual Organization

Bourguiba had a special attitude toward men of religion and a particular aversion to Zeitouna, the traditional religious establishment. Their sympathy for his political rival Salah Ben Youssef, assassinated in Frankfurt, Germany, in 1961, exacerbated that attitude. His unconditionally pro-Western politics created deep resentment among many people who remained deeply attached to their Arab-Islamic identity. On the other hand, the growing appeal of the left and trade unionism in the sixties and the seventies prompted some in the regime to strike at the left with the pan-Arabist religious trend under the cover of "Tunisification." In 1970 the Association for the Preservation of the Holy Koran was authorized. Despite its cultural character, this association showed since its first congress in 1971 a leaning toward "political Islam" and the ideas of the Islamic Brotherhood.

Certain political analysts in the West overlook the fact that fanaticism and the related use of violence are not a recent manifestation of fundamentalism and are not the result of non-recognition. They are instead inherent to such movements and are at the core of their discourse and organizational structures. Close scrutiny of those movements shows that violence becomes a corollary of every religious movement that strays from the promotion of purely religious values, gets politicized and appoints itself as she overseer of social life, the sole normative authority that decides what is heretical and what is righteous.[35]

One particular incident exemplifies the specific nature of "political Islam" contrary to the Zeitouna-type Islam known to Tunisians. Mr. Habib Mistaoui, one of the Zeitouna scholars, asked for clarification on the agenda of the Association for the Preservation of the Holy Koran, to put an end to its maneuvers and ambiguities. At a noted meeting in early 1972, Abdelfattah Mourou spoke on behalf of his companions saying, *"Our political line is that of rejection of all that is established, starting with society whose members we consider unbelievers even if they pray, fast, and go to Mecca for pilgrimage. The same goes for the ruling party which is one of the circles of heresy, and whoever adheres to it becomes a heretic."*

Its is reported that Sheik Mistawi lifted his trembling hand in anger and slapped Mr. Mourou before ordering all those present to leave.[36] This incident clearly shows the difference between the Zeitouna tradition, which puts a premium on the propagation of the faith and on public action on the one hand, and the fundamentalist Brotherhood type which favors secrecy and aims at denying the faith of society, toppling the regime and establishing an Islamic state. The first association created by the Movement was the cover for underground work and for the use of violence to seize power.

In 1972, the founding Congress for the Movement, also known as the Congress of the Forty, gave birth to the Islamic Group of Tunisia. The formation remained secret. The Congress decided that the Group be a section from a larger entity, and a local presence for the world-wide Islamic Brotherhood. In fact, the Islamic movements are not independent one from the other, nor are they different from one region to the other. They are cells of the same network and a continuum of a common thought. There were those who in 1988 advised us to treat our fundamentalist movement from the specific premise that it is less extreme than others. Such advice betrayed an ignorance of the nature of those movements and of the extent of their ties and solidarity. There are no moderates or extremists among them, simply a distribution of roles and a duality of discourse. They are not locally distinct movements but rather chapters of a global movement whose activities, financing and support are transnational.

One evidence for that is the allegiance given by the Islamic Group of Tunisia to the chief spiritual guide of the Muslim Brothers in Cairo during a pilgrimage in 1973. The Group found their inspiration in Hassan El Banna for organizational structure, and in Sayed Kotb for ideology. In their eyes Tunisian society had relapsed into paganism "regardless of prayer, fasting or pilgrimage to the holy places," and no one was eligible for Islam without membership in the Group.

Penitence became a fashion in the country. Sovereignty was the prerogative of God only, not of the people. Democracy was "idolatry" and the secularism of state "heresy." "Humanity," Sayed Kotb claims, "subscribes to either party: the party of god or the party of the devil, two distinctive and incompatible parties. The only thing that matters is faith, faith only, not parentage or genealogy or relation or country or gender." Tunisians may recall a time when the Group tried to invalidate any Muslim marriage contracted without the benediction of the organization.

This was the time that saw the appearance of *Al-Maarifa*, a magazine which reflected that mindset. In issue 8 (fifth year), Ghannouchi wrote: *"The very act of candidacy to a position in the Islamic state is good enough for exclusion from the state. An Islamic society should have no electoral campaigns, only the Umma may recommend and invest the candidates it sees fit."*

The Islamic Group refused at that time to request a permit to function as a political party since they rejected the very notions of party and democracy. They believed in the existence of one Islamic society waging and winning a holy war against the heretical rest.

The Islamic Group indulged in intelligence and propaganda, preparing for holy war and the taking of power. Mosques were the site of recruitment and initiation. For this reason they pushed for the building of mosques inside public and private institutions, inside factories and schools and universities and barracks. It did not matter what shape the mosques took, what mattered was their existence as organizational bodies and tentacles for recruitment and mobilization. The educational system and youth were a special target for the Group in those early days. Mohamed Mzali, who was Minister of Education and later Prime Minister, opened the door for them with the Tunisification and Arabization of education. The fundamentalists infiltrated the educational system with their ideas and methods under this cover, seeking to replace rationalism with dogmatism, to inculcate Islamist ideology, and to recruit their partisans as teachers—all this in the name of Arabization and Tunisification. Mzali calculated that he might need their support in his struggle for the succession against his competitors among the President's court, and in his confrontation with the trade union and the left. Mohamed Sayah, who was secretary-general of the ruling party at that time, seems to have taken a similar path, though for other reasons and for a short time.

The crisis of January, 1978, however, demonstrated that the Islamic Group remained isolated from the population, failing to control the streets. At the same time, the Iranian revolution demonstrated how street control could lead to power. The Group decided then to balance secrecy and openness. In 1981, they convened a congress to create a public body and a parallel secret body, both under a common leadership which Ghannouchi strongly sought to control. The dual organization led to two-faced double talk. It was necessary then to appear acceptable to public opinion, but the underground revolutionary activities were to continue.

The movement was reorganized accordingly and adopted the new name of the Movement of the Islamic Tendency. The leaders had to be trained in new methods of work and a new discourse, but violence remained one of the basic tenets of the movement, and this tenet had its men, its rules and its secret agencies.

In addition to the secret branch infiltrating the army, the police, the intelligence services, the parties, and the institutions of information, new bodies were born outside the Movement to carry on publicly whatever activities the Movement wanted to keep secret. We will return to some of those bodies with more detail later. The Movement, nevertheless, used all of them to conduct tactical negotiations and exert pressure on the regime for public concessions. The Movement put forth the idea that non-interaction with them would create even more extremist trends. Taken in by this diversion, the West started distinguishing between moderates and hard-liners, and calling for a rapprochement with the "nice guys" so as to alienate the "bad guys." What the West forgot was that the moderates were moderates only in appearance, that every mantle hid a knife, that the whole matter amounts to a diversification of roles. The top leadership is one, and behind every nice word lurks a dangerous project aiming to establish a totalitarian state. Democracy, in the ideology of the Movement, is a way of life contrary to the Islamic way. Fundamentalist faith simply cannot accept the rules of the democratic game.

We know from experience that whoever attempted to co-opt the fundamentalists and pull the rug beneath their feet eventually discovered that they swallowed whatever was given them and asked for more. That was the case with Anwar Sadat, with Chedly Benjedid, even with Gamal Abdul Nasser, who came close to falling into their trap. Chedly Benjedid brought Mohamed El-Ghazali and Youssef El-Kardhaoui, both leaders of the Islamist movement in Egypt, to give Algeria what he genuinely believed to be the true version of Islam, the version that respects state legitimacy and checks the version of disobedience and violence. Actually, those individuals planted in Algeria the seeds of discord and the spirit of fanaticism, and widened the base of recruitment for dogmatic extremists. The fundamentalist mind is extremist by nature, and extremism breeds violence: a maelstrom that swallows whoever tries to stop it from the inside. It thrives on an internal dynamic of ever-increasing extremism: the more extremist, the more powerful inside the Movement. This has already been demonstrated by the succession of events after the Iranian "revolution." Where today are the moderates who were by the side of Khomeini before the revolution? Whoever indulges in double talk becomes ineffective inside his organization, and thereby loses the confidence of the base and the support of outside partners.[37]

Bourguiba had tackled the fundamentalist phenomenon from a security-based perspective only, which resulted in its successive comebacks. Striking recurrently at the Movement only postponed the crisis. Besides, the secret branch remained safe beyond the ear of the intelligence services or the reach of the police. The members of the Movement are expert at taking cover. They swear vows of secrecy on the Holy Koran. On several occasions a convicted person went back immediately to documents or explosives he had kept secret during interrogation, in order to return them to the organization.

The Movement of the Islamic Tendency in Tunisia sought to benefit from fundamentalist experience abroad. From the Sudanese model they learned how to infiltrate state agencies and institutions. The Iranian experience was a lesson in how to Islamize the streets so as to gain the widest amount of sympathy possible. They mobilized all means to gain support, from sports to scouting, to culture, to information, to art. Didn't we in Tunisia witness weddings celebrated with popular songs that carried a politicized, fundamentalist content on the pretext of counteracting the "dilution of art"?[38] The movement also infiltrated some barracks and state institutions through their mosques. The daybreak prayer was considered the litmus test for the readiness of new recruits, and the best occasion for recruitment. The easiest infiltration, however, occurred in the educational system where the techniques of brainwashing were used, where dogmatism and irrationalism were inculcated, where values were dichotomized between what is permitted and what is forbidden, where people were categorized as either believers or heretics. Alms were mobilized to fund the movement, and so were some windfalls from oil revenues. Terrorist networks were created, and experts at document counterfeiting were employed, their stars still living

31

in Europe, in Spain, Germany and France, basking in asylum for their "political struggle"!

None of this would have been possible without the effective complicity of Mohamed Mzali, then Prime Minister. After the bread riots of January 1984, Mzali sensed his weakness and sought the support of the fundamentalists. He made their infiltration easier by opening public channels to them. They organized the founding congress of the General Union of Tunisian Students, which was their active nucleus not only in the universities but also in all mobilization activities and "disciplinarian" operations, using violence and acid. Mzali also annulled "Circular 108," which outlawed religion-related dress in schools, and managed with the mediation of third parties to win amnesty from Bourguiba on the basis of a "conciliatory letter" addressed to him by the movement and signed by Abdelfattah Mourou, July 4, 1984.

Foreign embassies invited the fundamentalists on national day celebrations and for debates. The movement responded eagerly to the invitations in order to gain foreign support—a much needed cover. Its rhetoric, which used to describe Western governments as the "forces of evil and hegemony," now called them "the people of the (Holy) book."

The dual organization and two-faced double talk of the Movement eventually caused dissension over leadership. A congress was convened in 1984 at Soliman to settle the issue. Seventy leaders were invited; it is reported that they met with veils on their faces. To unify their rhetoric they set up a legal department within the movement designed to harmonize their resolutions with Islamic jurisdiction. This meant that the opportunity for interpretation was eliminated even within the Movement itself, and that discussion and debate were no longer possible. The movement, with Ghannouchi behind it, thus reclaimed for itself the sole right of deciding what is and what is not compatible with Islamic jurisdiction in all aspects of life. The congress debated a document of extreme fanaticism, later known as *"The Ideological Vision and Principles of the Movement,"* to be used as the criterion in distinguishing between faith and heresy. They thereby identified political opposition to their agenda, not on the basis of its being wrong opinion, but on the basis of heresy, not on the basis of mismanagement but on the basis of sinfulness. By and large, you were not a believer until you subscribed to the terms of that document, and the movement reserved the right to deny your faith.

In the summer of 1986, Bourguiba dismissed his Prime Minister, Mohamed Mzali, in the middle of a social and economic crisis. The movement thus lost a major public supporter, and began to consider confrontation by weighing options for seizing state power. One major option was to activate its public front into street disturbances, so as to confuse and mislead the regime and give its special secret branch a free hand. While Ghannouchi pretended to freeze his activities, Karkar embarked on a tactic of incessant provocation to create tension in all sectors, with the aim of persuading all parties at home and abroad that the key to stability was no longer in the hands of the regime but in those of the Movement. The special secret branch was ready to carry out the plan for a coup, and the Movement set November 8, 1987 as the deadline for execution. In the final days of planning, a *fatwa* was decreed to justify the killing of fellow Muslims. The *fatwa* stated that these had become heretics for defending a heretical regime, making their assassination legitimate.

The execution of the coup was preceded by a series of daily street riots, arson in key institutions, the use of acid on opponents, and the murder of the Imam of the mosque in Le Kram. Prison walls at the time were easily permeable, so that the leaders of the Movement, including Ghannouchi himself, were able to issue instructions and lead operations.

The moment was ripe, they thought, to seize power. By Friday, November 6, the execution of the coup was underway. Karkar was so confident in success that his only worry was about missing his share of the bounty: from his hideout in London, he asked Essaied Ferjani to exhort the executors of the coup to "do what the Prophet's disciples did at the Battle of Badr, that is to be ruthless with the enemy but selfless in victory." This is why the event of November 7, 1987 was truly a salvation and a re-birth for Tunisia. On that day, the country leaped over the threat of a stifling totalitarianism.

The *Nahdha* Movement, like all cult movements, appeals to the ingenuousness of people by playing up to their faith and exploiting their inclinations. It also has a capacity for brainwashing and promises spiritual salvation to marginal persons and delinquents. They capitalize on the solemnity of mosques, where they deliver sermons and organize debates, to inspire them with the message they need and with the spiritual food they lack. They also possess the skills, as well as the methods and rituals, commonly applied to enslave people spiritually, and use them as time-bombs primed for explosion on demand. Court investigations of some of their members have demonstrated how innocent children have been submitted to delicate brainwashing just because they were young, naive, impressionable, lacking in judgment and unable to spot sinister political intentions behind the cover of religiosity. Once awakened by the trial experience, those children expressed their deep resentment for the Movement and its secret leadership, and started to militate against it by shaking its partisans out of their unconsciousness and misguidedness.

The new regime thus faced a double challenge: to build, but also to contain those who would destroy. The immediate period following the Change was particularly trying. Up until 1991, Tunisia encountered initial difficulties in meeting various needs and dealing with the problematic legacy of the previous years. It also faced other difficulties, uncovering fundamentalist coup schemes, and reversing the growing wave of sympathy the Movement had managed to gain during the previous regime. Tunisia also had to stem growing pressure from the extreme left and from pan-Arab nationalist groups loyal to certain Arab leaders. New organizations had by then emerged on the political scene after *Nahdha's* secret branch had been exposed. These organizations rejected double talk and advocated openly their intention to establish an "Islamic state" and to fight the heretical society. Among those organizations were: The Islamic Liberation Party,[39] the Islamic Front,[40] the Movement for Social Change,[41] the Islamic

Group,[42] the Group for Inquisition and Exile,[43] the Group for the Propagation of the Message,[44] the Martyr's Movement,[45] and the Disciples of the Truth.[46] There also emerged other organizations of the extreme left, in addition to the Tunisian Communist Workers' Party[47], the Revolutionary Marxist Communist Party, and the Nationalist Democratic Militants Party, as well as other pan-Arab organizations loyal to foreign states such as the Arab Revolutionary Committees.[48]

Though the extremist left-wing and pan-Arab organizations never really threatened the regime as such, they nevertheless were an obstacle to democratic harmony by preventing the rise of the moderate left and of the Arab nationalist movement, two genuine trends on the Tunisian political map.

These movements did not all operate individually and with internal resources alone, but also received foreign support in a variety of ways from the East as well as from the West. That support came in the form of sympathy, media coverage, and even defense in the name of "human rights." The *Nahdha* Movement, specifically, enjoyed great support from foreign governments that were themselves unaware of the danger it represented. Those governments granted it funds, promises of recognition as a full-fledged political party, and visas to that effect, in exchange for participation in wars in Afghanistan and elsewhere, for mediation with other extremist movements, and for pledges not to harm those governments' interests.

Democracy Free from Fundamentalism

Tunisia went through very hard times in 1990 and 1991, like a boat against the current. Foreign governments did not realize the danger of fundamentalist movements, and for various reasons could not see why those movements were denied a permit as a political party. Foreign officials and academics frequently confronted the Tunisian government with the issue of recognizing those movements. With a few exceptions, most of them felt that giving them recognition would diminish their influence, that they would be better allowed to function openly within the system, rather than secretly outside it. In any case, they believed that extremism would be absorbed and marginalized by the democratic mechanism. In Tunisia, too, this opinion was shared by some who later changed their minds in the light of subsequent events. The positions of many foreign governments, academics and scholars also changed after the Gulf war and after extremism had moved from the Middle East and south of the Mediterranean to nest in Europe and strike in New York and Paris. Tunisia responded to that pressure with an effort at persuasion, but at times chose to remain silent when it felt that the foreign interlocutor was motivated by self-interest, seeking to drive extremism away into political experiments in laboratories like Tunisia.

We in Tunisia had two things to say to those people:

First: Fundamentalist movements are anti-democratic and anti-dialogue by nature. They are totalitarian cult movements.

Whoever adhered to them was considered a believer, and whoever disagreed with them became a heretic. Faith could not be swallowed up and digested by

34

democracy, nor broken up and marginalized by the democratic process. They are movements which do not express an opinion, rather which fight for a faith they have distorted with a bizarre political content. Sovereignty for them is not the prerogative of the people, but of God alone. The distinction between moderates and extremists among them is irrelevant. Characterized by dual organization and double talk, they aim at one and the same object, and that end justifies the means.

Second: These movements are not local; they do not limit their activities to one country, in order to escape containment.

They operate across many countries to defend a "faith" and impose a "conviction" which they have distorted into a totalitarian system. No single democracy could absorb them, since their branches reach out abroad for funds, training, mobilization, and activation. The harder one tries to contain them in one place, the more they proliferate. Foreign intelligence services have now learned this lesson pragmatically, as have politicians in Algeria, Egypt, Jordan and elsewhere.

This is why Tunisia has remained on alert despite the withdrawal of fundamentalism as a threat and its rejection by society as a whole.

Tunisia has insisted on entering the democratic age without the involvement of fundamentalism, despite the opposition of other governments and of the international community in general at that time. The fundamentalists, who had focused on Tunisia as a launching board for their presence in the region, have failed to impose themselves as a party in the equation. Tunisia has therefore managed to establish a transparent democracy free of the extremism of fundamentalists. The transition to pluralism started with difficulty, as internal pressure was compounded with real external pressure. Faced with these challenges. Ben Ali opted for a new climate, where local concern with totalitarian fundamentalism becomes regional. That climate requires the cooperation of all concerned governments, since a local conflict south of the Mediterranean may well become a larger conflict north of the Mediterranean and threaten religious coexistence and international peace. Ben Ali has also demonstrated that the struggle is not with a movement but with a dangerous, extremist ideology that threatens human values.

Creating the New Climate

The new regime in Tunisia has been anxious to create a new political climate that breaks with the stifling atmosphere of the previous regime's final years. Ben Ali knew how to meet the real needs of Tunisians, and demonstrated an accurate awareness of the deep aspirations of all social groups, the elite as well as the man in the street, the rich as well as the poor.

Ben Ali has enabled Tunisians to regain confidence; this was perhaps the most important achievement of the Change. He has restored their optimism after years of defeatism and doubt.

Since the early 1970s Tunisia had lived on a day-to-day basis, while the people pondered their country's fate after Bourguiba. Political competition was reduced to a member of individuals and groups killing one another to inherit power. One former Prime Minister used to confide to his closest associates that his "political program consisted only in staying in office" until Bourguiba was gone. Whenever politics was the subject of conversation at the law school or at academic conferences, we felt the isolation and withdrawal of the regime and the general indifference to politics. The regime appeared to agonize while courtesans competed ruthlessly to inherit power from an aging leader.[49]

In this context, the November 7 Change was crucial in breaking with a previous model and a dangerous mentality, in creating a new climate and breathing a new life of optimism and confidence in the Tunisian people. Evidence of this appeared in opinion polls carried out by the Social Research Department for a study of family life in Tunisia (1993). Asked to compare the living standards of this and the former generations, 51.3% said that the present standards were better, 11.1% said that life was harder, 12.5% said that life had changed, and 8.4% felt no difference.

Asked *"How do you see your child's future?"*, 76.1% were optimistic, 18.8% were half optimistic, and only 15.7% were pessimistic for various reasons. Asked *"What bodies are capable of defending your interests?"*, 56.3% said the state (a good indicator for the social confidence in the regime as a whole), 9.6% said the trade unions, 0.7% said the associations, 0.8% said the parties, etc.

Tunisians have also regained the desire to participate in and contribute to building the country after years of resignation and indifference. Politics was no longer the monopoly of a closed circle inside the party or the state.[50] Politics has become everybody's concern, something to be shared, and a public forum. Suffice it to consider the popular attendance at debates in the first year since the Change, or the fora for political dialogue which the president had called for in preparation for his future program. Observers could no longer tell government officials from the opposition, or distinguish among the various opposition parties. Many new elites came forward to express their vision of tomorrow's Tunisia.

The new climate has inspired a sense of belonging, patriotism, and pride in contributing to the renewal process. I do not exaggerate when I say that Tunisians in the final days of the old regime were embarrassed to speak of their government in public fora, what with the irresponsibility of a president hostage to changing his mind overnight, and who dismissed a government only to re-install it, while the population laughed at the soap opera of weekly nominations and dismissals.

Tunisia's determined choice of a free economy, free enterprise and legitimate rewards after the reign of hesitation, has stimulated a new enthusiasm for work. The age-old Tunisian ingenuity and instinct for opportunity and commerce, harking back to the maritime empire of Carthage, emerged again.

I believe that the renewed confidence in the regime, the optimism, the new opportunities for work and prosperity,[51] have given the greatest impetus to economic growth and account for Tunisia's leap in development, as will be seen later.[52]

Let us review the practical measures that have been taken to consolidate the new climate in Tunisia. Far from being comprehensive, this review will focus on the most important samples of national reconciliation and mobilization for the new social project.

On December 31, 1987, a general amnesty was decreed for some 405 prisoners, all followers of the *Nahdha* movement. On April 8, 1988, all the civil servants who had been dismissed for trade unionist activities were re-admitted to work.

On May 4 of the same year, an amnesty was decreed in favor of one of the leaders of the fundamentalist movement who had been sentenced on September 27 to hard labor for life. On August 18, a legal amnesty was granted to all those who had been sentenced for trade unionist activities.

On November 5, further prosecution was dropped against 70 members of *Nahdha's* security arm; these had been arrested on November 6, 1987 on the eve of implementing their plan to seize power. On November 6, 1988, the Tunisian League for Human Rights declared that there were no more political prisoners in Tunisia. The next day, on the first anniversary of the Change, the National Pact was signed. Drafted jointly by the social and political bodies, this document highlights the values and principles around which consensus exists, unites Tunisians and rejects whatever might divide them and obstruct the way to democracy. On July 3, 1989, a general amnesty was decreed in favor of several groups who had been sentenced before November 7, and others undergoing prosecution; this amnesty enabled them all to regain their political and civil rights.[53]

On December 29, 1987, the State Security Court, which did not guarantee a fair trial for defendants, was abolished, together with the State Prosecutor's office which used to be an instrument for interfering in the judicial process.

On November 26, 1987, two weeks after the Change, the Penal Code was amended to limit the period of police custody and guard against brutality at the preliminary interrogation, to have the Public Prosecutor notified of the detention immediately, to limit the initial custody period to four days and require authorization for any extension, and to allow post-custody medical examination on request. The new measures are revolutionary since there used to be no time limit to custody and no safeguards.[54]

The Penal Code was also amended to reduce the custody period ordered by the judge for the investigation, to limit the recourse to custody, and to provide for an automatic suspension of custody unless the investigating judge or the prosecuting office decides otherwise.

On November 4, 1988, a new code was issued to regulate prison life and prison procedures in conformity with United Nations standards. The same day, a decree was issued to restructure the prisons and spell out the rights and duties of prisoners.

Tunisia also adhered to most international agreements on human rights. Other agreements that have not been signed are in effect covered elsewhere.

Thus a network of commitments was generated, covering all areas of human rights, such as slavery, servitude, trade unionism, refugees, stateless persons, children, women, the struggle against racial discrimination and segregation.

Those international agreements were published in the Tunisian Official Gazette for effective implementation and citation by the pertinent authorities and courts. Their publication demonstrates Ben Ali's good will in implementing the law, providing safeguards to defendants, and protecting human rights in general.

The agreement to eliminate all forms of discrimination against women, for example, was adopted on July 12, 1985, but was not published in the Official Gazette until after the Change on November 25, 1991. Likewise, the international convention on cultural, social and economic rights was adopted on November 29, 1968, but was not published in the Official Gazette until November 4, 1991.

Tunisia was also ready to honor without any reservation the International Convention on Political and Civil Rights which had been adopted on November 29, 1968, and published in the Official Gazette on November 12, 1983.

More significantly, Tunisia was willing to comply to the terms of Article 41 pertaining to the mode of implementation of the convention by declaring on April 23, 1993, her readiness to accept international complaints on any alleged violations of the convention.

On July 11, 1988, a few months after the Change, Tunisia also adopted the agreement against torture and other forms of harsh, inhuman or degrading treatment or punishment. The agreement was published immediately after adoption on October 20, 1988. Tunisia had no reservations about the terms of the agreement, including Articles 21 and 22, which provide for a specialized commission to look into the complaints that any country may raise against another in the matter, or into the reports of torture or ill-treatment by individuals or on behalf of individuals under Tunisian jurisdiction. This reflects the self-confidence of the regime and the transparency of its projected human rights policy. Tunisia presented its first report on the implementation of the agreement on October 25, 1989.

Tunisia, it is important to note, presents to the United Nations and to the Organization of African Unity regular reports on the implementation of the agreements she has committed herself to honor. Tunisia has also replied to the individual complaints filed at the United Nations.[55]

The adoption of international agreements and their publication in the Official Gazette have for Tunisia a special significance. In the eyes of the Constitution, international agreements have precedence over internal legislation, and in case of conflict those agreements are implemented.

No one claims that the mere adoption of those agreements guarantees the protection of all rights and the respect of all freedoms. Abuses and arrests continue to happen, but they are not state policy. Those abuses are the action of individuals, and as such take place in all democracies, particularly in nascent democracies seeking to establish a healthy civil society and having, in order to do that, to block the way to movements of fanaticism and the violence they entail. Such violations did take place in Tunisia, prompting a presidential order to investigate them and take the necessary measures to stop the abusers.

That was in June 1991, and again in June 1995 when investigative commissions visited prisons, conducted interviews and wrote reports outlining responsibilities and suggestions to the president. As will be seen later, the civil servants in charge of implementing legislation are supervised regularly and discreetly to make sure they do not abuse power.

New laws also were adopted to improve the social and political climate. On February 27, 1989, the penalty of hard labor was abolished, and replaced with imprisonment for the same time period. On November 17, 1994, the penalty of rehabilitation employment, a sentence issued by administrative committees which did not protect the legal rights of the accused, was abolished.

Three new political parties were granted a permit: The Unionist Democratic Union on November 30, 1988, the Progressive Socialist Rally and the Social Party for Progress on September 12 of the same year.

Amnesty International opened an office in Tunis on April 12, 1988, the first of its kind in the Arab region. Ben Ali also decided to host the Arab Institute for Human Rights on March 23, 1989, while no other country in the region was willing to do so.[56]

The public feeling of security and safety at home and in the streets testifies to the new climate created by the new regime.[57] New laws were adopted reflecting the desired social model and organizing political life gradually to establish and protect the new model. The most significant law has to do with the regulation of political parties.

The New Law on Political Parties, or, Excluding the Ideology of Extremism

On May 3, 1988, only months after the Change, a new law on political parties came into being, bringing with it a forward-looking vision of the future political life and the desired social model in Tunisia.

The new law, which has not received enough attention by analysts,[58] is the cornerstone of Tunisia's political organization today and epitomizes one aspect of the transition from a one-party system to pluralism. After initial criticism by some foreign observers, the law became a model worthy of consideration.

The new law on political parties organizes pluralism on the basis of the following provisions which guarantee its success:

First, the party must uphold the republican character of the state, the principle of sovereignty of the people, and the achievements in the area of the law of personal status. A fundamentalist cult party can never meet those three conditions, for it denies the republican character of the state as well as the sovereignty of the people, favoring instead a theocracy that reserves government nominally to God, but actually to "theologians" who set themselves up as mediators of the faith and guardians for others.

Nor would fundamentalism safeguard Tunisia's achievements in the area of personal status which set it apart from many other countries in the region and are not to be given up, especially as regards the liberation of women and the protection of their civil rights in marriage, guardianship, child custody, etc. Women in Tunisia will not agree, for example, to a reduction in the minimum age of marriage, to a denial of their right to choose a husband, to polygamy, or to repudiation.[59]

Second, the party must not base its charter of principles or subsequent activities on religion, race, or region.

This provision is inspired by the principles of the United Nations and the constitutions of democratic countries which reject discrimination on the basis of religion, race, region, etc.

Further, it is not enough for a party merely to proclaim that it upholds these principles; it should put them into practice.[60]

Third, the party must reject all forms of violence and must not be based on extremism or discrimination. Again, this condition is not satisfied by political movements of a fundamentalist inclination, which are by definition extremist in the defense of their beliefs, which reject dialogue and negotiation about what they consider unquestionable divine decrees, and which view themselves as the bearers of a message that has to be propagated even by force.

The true objective of this law is to guarantee effective pluralism at this crucial transition juncture following the collapse of the one-party system.

The political objective is to exclude extremist ideology which, if permitted to appear, would threaten to swallow up the existing democratic opposition or thwart its progress, would monopolize dissidence and absorb opposition, and eventually offer itself as the only alternative to the ruling party. Its rigid stance and its threat to the future of society would in turn force the ruling party to be equally rigid. Their competition thus becomes a ruthless confrontation that wipes out all other opposition and disperses the moderate center, which is the foundation of any democratic society.

The political scene would then be torn between two forms of one-party rule, an old one and a new one, both bad choices but the second one more dangerous because it propels society into a totalitarian system and postpones democracy ad infinitum.

Tunisia's policy in this respect is not unprecedented in the history of democratic countries. For had Germany not been lax in stopping the Nazi movement in the aftermath of the First World War, humanity might well have been spared the sufferings of the Second World War. The same goes for Italy and Japan. Today, the French National Front which, democrats point out, has lately swelled in numbers in an unusual way, has rallied the moderate right around its views, has exploited the social divisions resulting from unemployment, massive immigration, the moral disorientation of the young and the insufficient measures for their counseling and cultural integration. And unlike Tunisia, Algeria initially opted for the recognition of all parties, including those that do not believe in democracy. Only later did Algeria try to remedy the situation by outlawing all parties based on religion.

Such was also the case in Egypt.

Like racist movements, fundamentalist movements adopt a totalitarian ideology and a hysterical discourse. They refuse to share power, because government is for them nothing but applying *Shari'a* law, which is the prerogative of the theologian who, alone, can interpret the word of God and apply it to society.

Their true political views, which they are today anxious to conceal for tactical reasons, consider democracy a heresy and opposition a sacrilege. They present other interpretations of this sort, with no room for questioning, while public questioning is the basis of theological interpretation and the *raison d'être* of true theologians.

They set themselves up as the sole authorities who may accuse people of apostasy and atheism, who may grant faith certificates, and thus may revoke the right to citizenship and in some regimes, even the right to life.

Rather than men of religion in the usual sense, they are politicians cloaked in religious robes.

That is why political discourse in Tunisia today has adopted the tenet that religion is for everyone and cannot be monopolized by any movement, that mosques are the houses of God and not arenas for political activism. The state, as a national authority, has the duty to respect, safeguard and protect Islam. Hence, Ben Ali has rehabilitated Islam, reinstituted the call to prayer, accorded special attention to religious celebrations, and restored to its former glory Zeitouna as a mosque and a university.

Special care for mosques and imams was taken. New religious institutions in the form of neutral associations took on the teaching of true Islam and began to contribute to the writing of text-books and children's stories so that the young may he raised with true Islamic values, free of distortion and indoctrination.[61]

At this point, it is necessary to emphasize a few things which illustrate Ben Ali's genuine belief in Tunisia's Islamic identity and his wish to restore Islam to its former solid socio-cultural standing, on the grounds that the best rampart against fanatical Islam is true Islam, and the best defense against fundamentalism will come from genuine Muslims and genuine theologians.[62]

As early as November 28, 1987, two weeks after the Change, regular calls for prayer were broadest on radio and TV. In the words of Abdelmajid Ben Hamda, *"There is in the call to prayer something that moves Muslims,"*[63] a constant and regular reminder of their Islamic culture and identity, a continuing direct bond between them and God without any mediation whatsoever.

After a long period of disputes with other Islamic countries, Tunisia adopted the *Hijra* Calendar along orthodox lines. Sighting of the moon, as well as calculation, are now used to determine the start and finish of Ramadan for all Tunisians, in accord with the rest of the Muslim world. During the previous regime, it will be recalled, the confirmation of those dates used to be an occasion for fanatics to incite dissent and feed hatred for the regime on the pretext that the dates were not aligned with the rest of the Muslim world. Bourguiba, they used to say, wanted to obliterate their identity and sever the bonds of unity with other Muslims by tampering with the highly symbolic month of fasting.

The Zeitouna regained its former glory after thirty years of marginalization and dissipation. The oldest university in the Islamic world, the Zeitouna was established in 774 (116 AH) inside the Zeitouna mosque.

It was the lantern of tolerant Sunni Islam, boasting the Malakite Theological School as one of the most prestigious schools of Islamic theology and law. To the Zeitouna befell the task of fighting and stopping the invasion into Tunisia of Shi'ism, isolation and other external forces. Imam Sahnoun Ibn Said drove them away from Okba Ibn Nafaa mosque in Kairouan lest they became the source of division among the tolerant Muslims of Tunisia.[64] The Zeitouna also produced many scholars and philosophers, like the philosopher-historian Abdul Rahman Ibn Khaldoun in 1406 (808 AH), author of world-famous *"Prolegomena"* (*Al-Muqaddima*) in sociology; and the pioneer of the science of human geography, Al Barzali in 1438 (841 AH); Abdelaziz Thaalbi in 1920, forefather of the Democratic Constitutional Rally; Tahar Haddad, pioneer of the liberation of women; poet Abul Kacem Chebbi, who sang for freedom and nationalism early in this century, and many others. The Zeitouna University today is returning Islam to its true radiance, and contributing by its distinguished teaching to the updating of religious discourse.

Added to this was the enrichment of the Higher Islamic Council and its advisory role in safeguarding Islam from dissipation and closure. Among other things, the Council looked into the programs of Islamic education for children and similar issues pertaining to education and growth with values of true Islam.

Attention then turned to the construction and equipment of mosques. More than a thousand small and large mosques, a quarter of the total national number, were built after the Change. Memorization and reading of the Koran were promoted with a law on editions of the Koran promulgated on August 18, 1988, a Presidential Award for Memorization and Recitation of the Koran instituted in April 1990, and the Noble Koran read non-stop at the Zeitouna Mosque every single day of the year, by order of Ben Ali. Never before had the Zeitouna seen such care taken of the Koran.

Koranic schools were also safeguarded against exploitation for the indoctrination of youth and a special effort was made by Tunisia to renew religious discourse and to organize regular seminars, lectures, and study groups for Imams and preachers. Daily banquets given for the needy and the disabled every year in Ramadan testify to real compassion and solidarity, and lead Islam into a new dimension away from political exploitation. At many of the banquets Ben Ali was there to dine and speak with the guests and struck a responsive chord in everyone, especially the poor.

Anyone who has witnessed the struggle for true Islam during the initial period after the Change (1988 to 1991) cannot have failed to notice two twin attributes in the conduct of Tunisians: First, that Tunisians, whether they practice it or not, are deeply devoted to Islam, because, for Tunisia and many other Arab countries, it is the expression of identity; and they are easily moved by religious discourse, for Islam is a faith deeply rooted in the collective consciousness.

Second, that Tunisians reject the political exploitation of Islam, because they all consider themselves Muslims, whether they observe Islamic rituals or whether they choose not to do so for the moment. They reject the idea of a priestly guardian, of a theologian with a monopoly on religious understanding, or of a political movement that lays claim to religion, declares them heretics however and whenever it wishes to do so, or grants them faith certificates.[65]

In this respect, it is notable that a Department of Social Research opinion poll on the attitudes of Tunisians toward tourism (1994) shows a clear rejection on their part of the politicization of religion and of violence. Only 6% of them thought tourism incompatible with our customs—a proportion that is a little smaller than the 1989 fundamentalist electoral base. As for the violence against tourists in Egypt by the armed group, Tunisians were against it, 83.5% to 2.3%, while just 6.5% felt they could understand it.

As noted before, in 1972, the *Nahdha* movement, then a minor Islamic group in its beginnings, refused to apply for a party political permit, on the grounds that affiliation to parties was against the law of God, that democracy was "a new paganism," and that government was the prerogative of God alone. It then shifted its ground and put forward a public leadership to win over support. It had decided to swim with the tide, constituted a party ostensibly to compete with the other parties, and adopted a tactical rhetoric opposed to its initial line in a bid for public sympathy and support and to make itself out to be a victimized group seeking no more than a place for itself and a voice along with the other voices.[66]

Following the Change, on February 19, 1989, the *Nahdha* dropped the reference to Islam in its name and started to call itself by the new name in the belief that that would secure for it conformity with the new law on political parties, with the National Charter, and with all the principles agreed by the institutions of civil society, specifically the non-monopolization and the non-politicization of religion as well as the commitment to an unmediated relationship with God as specified by the Koran, the religion that belongs to all and whose protection falls to the state.

The movement retained its ideology of declaring its opponents heretics, however, and despite the new regime's extension of its policy of reconciliation to it and the inauguration, on January 8, 1990, of *Al-Fajr* (*The Dawn*) newspaper as the voice of the movement's views,[67] events were later to reveal that it had been simultaneously pursuing the tactics of double talk and secret parallel organization.

Even as it had the benefit of implicit recognition and public relations with the government and with the democratic parties, even as it was participating in the legislative elections in April 1989 through the lists of independent candidates,[68] the movement proceeded to hold a secret conference in Sfax attended by those among its members who had been released or had escaped detection. The items on the agenda of the conference were to devise a secret plan and concrete options to seize power. While Ghannouchi was proclaiming, after his release from prison, that "God has brought this Muslim country out of darkness when He sent it someone who exalts Islam," that "God has blessed Tunisia with a new dawn," and that he "wishes to thank everyone who has a part in this, particularly the Maker of November 7," he was actually orchestrating the security group which was to infiltrate the army and the security forces, and working with it on the preparation of a coup. The old scenario was re-set in motion as the public figures in the leadership moved to divert attention while the secret branch carried on with its underground havoc in order to snatch power.

When the results of the legislative elections of April 2, 1989 dashed the hopes of the *Nahdha* of emerging as the only alternative to the Democratic Constitutional Rally, and to rally dissent round it, it changed its tactics no longer to rely on public opinion for political presence in democratic institutions. Leadership roles were then redistributed and the activities of the secret branch received priority.

As noted earlier, Ghannouchi then fled the country, as did other leaders, to await at a distance the success of their planned operations. One initial plan devised in October 1990 was to wage a campaign of "harassment" against the regime with the circulation of leaflets and the writing of graffiti as a prelude to storming through the streets so as to confront the security forces and to burning down public institutions until the army was called in, making room for the military branch to move about barracks and gain control of the state machinery; while a second so-called emergency plan was to create a constitutional void by assassinating key political leaders and invading the streets in a massive revolt designed to topple the government.[69]

It is therefore easy to appreciate the double responsibility placed upon the government, for it did not only have to build but also protect what it built. That is why it drew on the sociological findings affecting the community to chart and maintain a course of action, both clear and resolute, designed to contain the fundamentalist movements and determine the means to confront them.

The vital ingredient of the strategy was to break the bond between the *Nahdha* and its sympathizers by exposing the real, exclusive designs behind their rhetoric to public opinion, and adopting the slogan *"All For Islam and None for its Monopolists"* to inspire political action. The strategy also sought to lay bare the dangers ensuing from a manipulation of Islam that destroys its transparency, vitality, and cohesiveness and turns it into a monopoly of one group which then subjects it to distortion and peddling, and uses it to sow division where it had been a rallying, unifying force.

This rhetoric with its slogans was later to be taken on by other countries anxious to face up to extremist fundamentalist groups. By 1993, with just five years gone by, it was adopted by the U.S. State Department when its spokesmen and renowned experts started asserting that their hostility was not to Islam but to individual Islamic movements in other countries. And only a few years later, the Gulf countries too rather changed their tone when, in the wake of the Gulf war, which was the moment of truth to put to the test the fundamentalist movements' intentions, the governments of those countries stopped consistently supporting Islamic movements and started discriminating between the true Islam that should prevail and political movements that exploit it for other ends. Across the board, they accept the propagation of Islam as a religion of the community, but reject its exploitation as a means of access to power. They accept social Islam, so to speak, and reject political Islam. That is why Kuwait along with other Gulf countries enacted laws to control the funding of associations and follow up on the *Zakat*, or Islamic alms-giving, so as to prevent extremism feeding on it by the backdoor.

It is then no exaggeration to say that Tunisia pioneered a political discourse with a style and slogans that came to gain ground in the whole region.

All this goes to show that the fight against fundamentalism is not a task that falls to the state alone but a collective process that calls for the involvement of all the community, and that is the second step in Ben Ali's plan.

Multilateral Action, or, from the Fight of the State to the Fight of the Community

To secure the transition to pluralism, Tunisia adopted one constant strategy in involving all the institutions of civil society in the fight against fundamentalism rather than simply relying on the effort of the state. With a society marked for decades by political unilateralism and utter dependence on the state, that objective was all the more difficult to achieve. Yet, the government managed to change the course of events and turn the fight against extremism and lawlessness from a state fight to one involving all the community.

Ben Ali chose a multilateral action with a collective mobilization, not just of the conventional security, defense, and judiciary apparatus of the state, but also of all the parties and associations, coupled with a deployment of the influence of the national elites.[70] The action did not just address cases that broke the law but combined it with a preventive approach to root out the causes of extremism by reducing pockets of deprivation, stemming the spread of poverty and unemployment, and laying the foundations of an effective prosperity based on free initiative.

It worked to bring about an enlightened reform of educational institutions and curricula, and to fill cultural and information gaps to best serve the new democratic line. It also cautioned against the consequences of disruption or lawlessness.

Punitive measures are indispensable because offenses cannot be glossed over and because the application of the law is not a right the organs of the state enjoy, but a duty society demands. Indeed, society, through its representatives, votes for the laws that everyone has to observe and abide by. And more than all others, the democratic system is called upon to respect the rules of the game by obeying the law, and to install a robust state capable of imposing the standards of fair competition on everyone. The absence of that respect flies in the face of dialogue and stifles opposition. Difference then turns into dissidence and competition into a blood feud.[71]

For these reasons, the organs of the state were thorough and commendable in fulfilling their part. Accordingly, those who carried on their activities in banned groups were brought to trial, whether they were operating within the *Nahdha* or within offshoots it subsequently spawned in an attempt to evade suspicion of violence; the said offshoots came in a variety of shapes: the Vanguards of Sacrifice (*Tala'i Al Fidaa'*), the Vanguards of Martyrdom (*Tala'i Al*

Shuhada'), the Vanguards of Righteousness (*Tala'i Al Haqq*), the Party of Liberation (*Hizb Al Tahrir*), the Islamic Front (*Al Jabha Al Islamiyya*), and so on. All these small groups had leaders who broke away in name from the *Nahdha* to carry out acts of violence and destruction. If they failed the *Nahdha* could disavow them, and if they succeeded, it could profit by their success to toughen its public stance and gain more bargaining leverage with the authorities as well as more credibility with public opinion.

During the period that saw the arrests, from 1989 to 1992, the authorities in Tunisia came under fire both at home and abroad. From within loomed the threat of this web of extremists leading back into foreign networks of organization, training, and funding, and enmeshing embattled security officers, who often faced harrying arrests as the armed members of these groups resorted to force against them. From without came the backing certain governments afforded these groups, who profited especially from the aforementioned publicity by human rights organizations.

Security officers took an eminent part in putting a stop to the acts of violence and terror perpetrated by extremist elements against the public at large, striking in homes, schools, and work places and in the street. In the face of an exacerbating confrontation, security officers received instructions ordering them to obey the law and refrain from abuses. The Minister of the Interior issued three circulars: one on December 16, 1991, enjoining chiefs of police stations to display, in their offices, the text of the vow taken by Interior Security officers; a second on December 24, only days later, ordering them to publicize the United Nations Code of Conduct for Law Enforcement Officers[72]; and a third on February 24, 1992, on signing the commitment to respect human rights and public liberties.[73] Recent figures from the Ministry of Justice for the period January 1, 1988 to March 31, 1995 show that the number of abuse-related cases stood at 302. Only five of those had to do with the use of force to obtain a confession and seven with entering private property without warrant, while around half the cases were connected with ill-treatment committed while on duty. So, the figures demonstrate the regime's commitment to full compliance with the law. Top security commanders for their part did their best to prevent any abuses.

That commitment is what made Tunisia's security action quite different from many other countries who faced such difficulties with a drastic security response and acts of counterviolence such as forcible disappearances, the practice of torture, and killing on arrest to avoid complicated trials.[74] That only started a vicious circle of terrorism and counterterrorism, fueled already existing anger, and widened rather than contained the scope of the conflict, precipitating society into a form of civil war. I personally recall how Ben Ali would emphasize this point, reminding the Minister of the Interior on many an occasion that security officers can carry out their duties according to the law and professional standards, without resorting to brutality or ill-treatment. He would urge the government not to overlook abuses, and to strengthen disciplinary action and judicial prosecution with preventive steps by instilling rules of procedure for arrests and interrogations, teaching the principles of human rights at security officers' institutes, and posting the International Declaration of Human Rights in the doorways of police stations.[75]

Tunisia's judicial approach is also worthy of discussion and comment. At least in its initial assault on fundamentalism, this approach contrasts with that of many other countries—Egypt and Algeria, for example, as well as several established democracies. In fact, since the Change, never has Tunisia resorted to extraordinary trials, nor has it declared a state of emergency, as all violations committed by elements of extremist groups are tried as ordinary acts, before ordinary courts, on the basis of ordinary procedures. Nor has Ben Ali constituted extraordinary courts to hear crimes by extremists. Instead, he abolished the State Security Court, which, not being composed exclusively of judges and having different defense procedures and judicial hierarchy, could not guarantee a fair trial. According to usual procedure, all cases are still referred before the different penal courts throughout the Republic. Ordinary judges, without exception or special appointment, conduct trials, vindicating trust in their shared conviction of the threat of these movements and criminality of their activities, while in other countries terrorist cases are heard by special courts, or by judges who are carefully selected and protected from pressure or threats.

Even in France, among other established democracies, investigation and hearing of terrorist acts is confined to the courts of Paris, which have jurisdiction over the whole Republic. Algeria too followed the Egyptian model, but under President Liamine Zeroual normalized its handling of terrorist cases by confirming the jurisdiction of ordinary courts.

I have in fact suggested, in an interview with the former Algerian Minister of Justice, Mohammed Taqiyya, how Tunisia's approach does not single out terrorist crimes for special courts or districts or procedures and how it has worked instead to normalize such cases by involving all judges in examining them, not to attract the media attention these movements crave, nor present them with evidence they could latch on to in human rights circles, to claim their trials did not take place according to a normal, fair procedure.

To process these crimes, Tunisia enforces the same rules of procedure as those it follows with ordinary crimes, from the moment of arrest, to police custody, to court proceedings. By contrast, terrorist laws enacted in France, the United Kingdom, the USA, Germany, Italy, and many other countries subject terrorist crimes to stringent measures, with the safeguards granted to defendants reduced to enable the public prosecution and security officers to indict terrorists and courts allowed extensive powers to impose stiff penalties.[76]

Tunisia's commitment to treat as ordinary such crimes of organized fanaticism is best illustrated by the legislation on the period of custody, that is, the time when the suspect is detained by the police, leading to his appearance before the public prosecutor.

Two choices then arose: Either to extend the custody period for crimes of fanaticism and attendant terrorism and reduce it for ordinary crimes to 24 hours, the maximum required for preliminary questioning in such cases, or to retain the four-day period for all crimes. This latter choice was adopted, and

Basic Initiatives in Favor of Equality of the Sexes Before the Law

Ever since independence in 1956, Tunisia has developed a strategy aimed at achieving equality of the sexes. A constitutional and legal framework which highlights women's rights has greatly facilitated the way to equality of the sexes, especially thanks to the adoption of laws against sexual discrimination under the leadership of the authorities.

Having resolutely turned her back on the past, Tunisia has promulgated new laws on the family which prohibit polygamy and marriage without consent and install equal rights between men and women in the area of divorce. Women now have the right to pass their nationality on to their children when their husband is a foreigner.

Nowadays, in Tunisia, women waiting for a divorce have the right to custody of their children, whatever their age and sex. The civil code guarantees the right to contraception at a price accessible to all. Due to the promotion of family planning and a favorable legislative environment, fertility rates have gone down 50 percent in the last 20 years.

Besides legislation establishing the rights of women within the family, parallel legislation endeavors to achieve the same results in the economic sphere. The Tunisian civil code guarantees equality in the areas of inheritance, access to education, and the right to work. It recognizes women's right to manage property independently of their husbands.

Regulations prohibit discrimination in the areas of employment and salaries, encouraging the participation of women in the economy. Maternity leave and daycare centers contribute to the protection of women's right to work. In addition, professional training for women has been developed: some 86,000 women have benefited from it between 1986 and 1992. Thus, women's contribution to the active population has more than trebled, going from 6% in 1966 to 21% in 1989. The Tunisian women's movement, which comprises feminist organizations, research centers, and governmental bodies, has contributed to the social transformation assisted by the anti-discrimination laws. Members of those organizations have disseminated the information on these laws and participate in the debate on the advancement of women. The reforms quickly won general approval and are now well-established; practically, women of all social classes are in fact well-informed of their rights.

Women's activism is manifested in their increasing participation in decisions of a political nature. In 1994, 7% of returned Parliamentary representatives were women, the most important figure for all the region. At the local level women's representation is close to the world average of 14%.

Even if the Tunisian family statute does not give total equality to women in all aspects of their social life, it is notably advanced for some of those rights. Provisions of the Tunisian family statute and property law on sexual discrimination are in conformity with—or rather based on—traditional and religious values.

Sources CAWTAR 1994, CREDIF and Tunisia 1994

United Nations Development Program
Report on Human Development 1995

Original: French

though the custody period is not crucial for ordinary crimes and not sufficient to process organized crimes of fanatic terrorism, the four-day rule applies equally well to a con man who tried to swindle a tourist out of money and to a dangerous terrorist who detonated a device in a hotel discotheque. Yet, the terrorist operates not in isolation but within a full-scale organization. From the moment he joins the organization, he pledges confidentiality to his leaders, vowing not to divulge their secrets for at least the first few days of detention to allow his accomplices time to make their escape, elude suspicion, or remove incriminating evidence.

The only exception to that rule occurred in August, 1992, when, following its exposure as a clandestine faction of the *Nahdha*, a "Security Group" was tried in a military court, though legal experts would not regard this case as an exception. That is because for any defendant soldier or officer in a security or similar corps, as were leading elements in the defendants here, the law regulating military courts, taken to the letter from French legislation, refers jurisdiction to military courts on the grounds that the identity of the case as a whole should be preserved. And the military judiciary is not an exceptional but a specialized one, for the court is presided over by a civilian judge, the same court procedures are followed as those enforced in the ordinary judiciary, and appeals and reviews of judgments conform to the civilian model. What is more, defense rights were fully respected in the August, 1992, trial when testimony to the guarantees afforded to the defendants came from foreign observers in attendance.

Tunisia's judicial approach not only has the merit of addressing extremism from this angle. The legislature also sought, by an amendment of the Penal Code on November 22, 1993, to bring to account a new form of organized crime, namely incitement to fanaticism and instigation of hatred. These are crimes it treats as serious, terrorist ones, allowing no room for leniency in judgments and no less than half the prescribed sentence, thus limiting the applicability of extenuating circumstances. Behind this law lies a distinction between freedom of thought, which is unrestricted and absolute, and the right to propagate that thought, which is subject to restrictions to the extent that these secure the protection of society. That the individual may be extremist in his thinking, fanatic in his ideas, self-centered, isolated, and a hater of others is a right for which he can neither be prosecuted nor brought to trial. That is why in Tunisia today you still come across those who would show fanatic zeal in clinging on to Islam, performing rituals alien from the Tunisian world, with roots in Pakistan, Afghanistan, and elsewhere. Thus, one may encounter women covered in veils, men dressed in long gowns, beards as long as they care to grow them, and rituals unfamiliar in religious observances. Nevertheless, to seek to propagate, advocate, or incite to this kind of thinking is to perform a physical act that affects the whole of society and to fall foul of the law by committing a punishable crime.

The distinction between the right to freedom of thought and the right to propagate or advocate that thought still needs further comment. For Tunisia does not take ideological extremism or religious fanaticism, in and of themselves, to be crimes, but these do turn into crimes the moment a person engages in concrete, physical acts to propagate that ideology, for example by setting up or joining an organization, such as a party or an association, or funding its activities, or by holding meetings to foster that ideology, or by distributing leaflets or composing works. That is why all pronounced judgments, you will find, impose sanctions for physical acts such as affiliation to a banned association or an unauthorized party, funding banned activities, holding meetings, or possessing or distributing leaflets that advocate extremism and incite to fanaticism and the propagation of that ideology. Thus it is that there arose an as yet unresolved difference of opinion with Amnesty International, which to this day regards these as crimes of conscience with a political character. What Amnesty has so far failed to do, despite discussions and communications with its leadership, is appreciate the distinction between an individual's ideology or opinion, which remains a natural, absolute right that cannot be restricted, and physical acts that seek to propagate that ideology and that may be banned when society finds they threaten to harm its well-being and the progress of democracy. It is worth recalling here how Amnesty itself emerged as a humanitarian movement in the aftermath of World War II, primarily to protect humanity from the crimes of Nazism, the most heinous of crimes of fanaticism and hatred. So if Amnesty could cast its mind back a moment to that day, would it then deem Nazi acts an expression of freedom of opinion? Would it regard Nazi prisoners, had they been imprisoned in the 1920s and '30s, as prisoners of conscience?

One more notable feature of Tunisia's judicial process here is its exclusion of the term "terrorism" as grounds for judgments rendered, given the politicization and trivialization that have befallen this term, which has, so to speak, suffered from wear and tear, and lost the international consensus it once enjoyed. Instead, courts in Tunisia now, in accordance with the new law, make use of the terms *incitement to fanaticism* and *instigation of racial and religious hatred.*

Incidentally, the aforementioned amendment of the Penal Code did not contrive new, separate crimes, but merely gave a new designation to familiar ones—constituting an unauthorized party, holding meetings, distributing leaflets, or collecting funds without authorization—for which sentences grow stiffer where the purpose of such acts is to advocate fanaticism and incite religious or racial hatred.

By a new provision of an amendment of Article 313 of the Penal Code, Tunisia abstains from granting political asylum to those who have committed such crimes. Tunisia further declares, in Article 305, that she will prosecute and sanction before Tunisian courts any Tunisian who has on foreign soil committed crimes of incitement to fanaticism or racial and religious hatred, even where the country concerned does not in its legislation proscribe such acts. And that signals Tunisia's resolve to treat advocacy of fanaticism and incitement of racial and religious hatred as crimes against humanity.

Prosecution and sanction may be sought in any country, regardless of whether the acts are recognizable crimes under that country's law. Nor are such crimes regarded as political ones, as extradition is mandatory.

The point of all these details is that they complete the picture of Tunisia's policy on fundamentalist movements. For Tunisia happens to regard them as a menacing phenomenon, their organized criminal acts as akin to crimes against humanity, calling for the cooperation of all governments.

Neither does Tunisia hold with the view that theirs are crimes of conscience or political crimes. She, at first alone, worked energetically to prevail on other governments not to grant asylum to elements of such movements and to extradite them to their countries of origin where they can stand trial or serve their sentences.

Alone, again, stood Tunisia in seeking to convince human rights organizations of the need for wariness of these movements and to treat their members, not as victims of their political opinions, but as advocates of a pernicious ideology who are engaged in organized physical crimes and pose a real threat to the human rights movement the world over.

Tunisia's first success in its effort to win over consensus on the threat of these movements came perhaps in the United Nations, which was able to make the distinction between the right to freedom of thought, which is absolute, and the freedom to propagate that thought, which is restricted. It decided that the advocacy of ideas of fanaticism and hatred is a serious crime, not a crime of conscience.

The United Nations Working Group in charge of investigating arbitrary detentions had in fact received a complaint from one Ahmed Kahlaoui, who claimed he had been tried in Tunisia for his opinions and should therefore be released. On March 4, 1994, Ahmed Kahlaoui had proceeded to write and distribute a leaflet entitled "Death to the Murderous Zionists," where he says, *inter alia*, "After all, what manner of normalization can there be with these criminals who are welcomed on Tunisian soil as tourists, scientists, and singers, met with red-carpet treatment, made into citizens enjoying the right to nationality and to possession of land and wealth, who find the doors of the country flung wide open and concoct supposed sacred places as the [Jewish] Ghriba in Jerba...They offer them hospitality and press us night and day to show them tolerance and to favor closer relations between nations and cultures...?"

On March 8, 1994, Kahlaoui was brought to trial in accordance with Article 52 *bis* of the Penal Code, which sanctions anyone who sets out to incite fanaticism or racial or religious hatred, whatever the means used. On June 27 he was sentenced by the Court of First Instance to two years and eight months of imprisonment. On October 18, and on appeal from him, the Court of Appeal upheld the primary judgment.

After receiving the complaint, with backing by extremist movements of fundamentalism, and also by Amnesty International and other organizations, the UN Working Group came to the decision which reaffirmed that constraints upon freedom of expression as stipulated by Tunisian law for the purpose of sanctioning opinions and statements that advocate racial hatred do not contradict international standards, and especially Articles 19 and 20 of the International Convention on Political and Civil Rights.

Decision No. 12/1994 (Tunisia)

Communication addressed to the Tunisian Government on April 22, 1994. With reference to: Ahmed Kahlaoui on the one hand, and the Tunisian Republic on the other.

1. The Working Group on Arbitrary Detention, in accordance with its adopted working methods, in order to complete its mission with discretion, impartiality, and independence, has transmitted to the Government concerned the aforementioned communication of which it has been informed and which it has deemed admissible, with regard to a case of alleged detention which would have taken place in that country.

2. The Working Group notes with appreciation the information conveyed by the Government in question on the case which has been communicated to it, within the period of 90 days from the dispatch of the letter by the Working Group.

3. With a view to taking a decision, the Working Group has examined whether the cases under consideration come under one, or more, of the three following categories:

I. Either the loss of liberty is arbitrary, as it is evidently not possible to relate it to some legal base (such as detention in custody beyond the term of a sentence or in spite of an amnesty law).

II. Or the loss of liberty involves facts which are the subject of prosecution or a conviction relating to the exercise of rights and liberties protected by Articles 7, 13, 14, 18, 19, 20, and 21 of the Universal Declaration of Human Rights and by Articles 12, 18, 19, 21, 22, 25, 26 and 27 of the International Covenant on Civil and Political Rights.

III. Or a non-compliance with all or part of international standards on the right to a fair trial such as imparts to the loss of liberty, whatever it may be, an arbitrary character.

4. Given the allegations made, the Working Group welcomes with satisfaction the cooperation of the Tunisian Government. The Working Group has conveyed the answer of the Tunisian Government to the source from which the information originates, which has itself transmitted its comments on August 4, 1994. The Working Group estimates being in a position to take a decision on the facts and circumstances of the cases in question, taking into account the allegations made and the answer provided by the Government as well as by the source.

5. According to the latter, Ahmed Kahlaoui, aged 50, teacher and trade unionist, would have been arrested on March 4, 1994, and charged with illegal distribution of pamphlets (condemning the Hebron massacre) whereas he was peacefully exercising his right to freedom of thought and expression. His petition for release would have been refused and he would have been detained, since April 8, 1994, in the Tunis prison.

6. The Government, which confirms the date and circumstances of the arrest, adds the following information

- The pamphlets which the author has prepared at his home call for a confrontation with all Jews, in Tunisia as well as in all the other Arab countries, and for a boycott of all scientific conferences and meetings in which they participate.

Original: French

52

- He advocated, in addition, not to negotiate with Jews on the economic as well as on the political level, insisting particularly on the need, for the Tunisian people, to attack the Jewish community of Djerba.

- It is within this context that he has appeared before the Criminal Affairs Magistrate's Court, on March 8, 1994, for incitement to hatred between races, religions, and populations, as well as for the publication of pamphlets liable to jeopardize public order.

- After a succession of referrals on March 24 , March 31, and April 14, he was finally judged on June 27, 1994, and condemned to two years of prison accompanied with a fine of one thousand Dinars for incitement to racial hatred (Art. 52 bis of the Penal Code), and eight months of prison for publication of pamphlets with a fine of one hundred Dinars for violation of the provisions of copyright registration (Art. 12, 44, and 62 of the Code of the Press).

7. In its comments on the answer of the Government, received by the Working Group on August 4, 1994, the source estimates that it is a question of "a political prisoner" and calls for him to be granted a prompt and fair trial, "in accordance with the rules of international law."

8. Given the above elements, the Working Group finds that on the basis of the position adopted by the Committee on Human Rights (Petition 104/1981, JRT and WG. Party C. Canada) on April 6, 1983, the restrictions introduced by the Tunisian law on freedom of thought with a view to combating the dissemination of racist ideas or comments, in the case in point being violently anti-Semitic, are compatible with the standards of international law and notably with Articles 19 and 20 of the International Pact on Civil and Political Rights according to which:

- Article 19, paragraph 3: "The exercise of liberties provided for by paragraph 2 defining freedom of expression in this Article entails special duties and special responsibilities. Consequently, it may be subjected to certain restrictions which should nevertheless be stated explicitly by law and which are necessary:

a) the respect of the rights or reputation of others.
b) the safeguard of national security, public order, public health or morality."

- Article 29, paragraph 2 : "All calls for national, racial, or religious hatred which constitute incitement to discrimination, hostility, or violence are forbidden by law".

9. In the light of what precedes, the Working Group returns the following decision:

The detention of which Ahmed Kahlaoui has been the subject does not fall within any of the three categories of applicable Principles for the examination of cases submitted to the Group, and notably not within category II, inasmuch as incitement to racial hatred is a crime not an opinion. Therefore, the detention of Ahmed Kahlaoui is hereby declared non-arbitrary.

Adopted on September 28, 1994.

Paragraphs from the Decision of the United Nations Working Group on Arbitrary Detention
No. 12/1994 (Dated September 28, 1994)

Original: French

Law No. 112 of 1993, dated November 22, 1993, as a Supplement to the Penal Code (1).

On behalf of the people,

After the approval of the Chamber of Deputies,

The President of the Republic proclaims the following law:

Unique Article

Appended to Section III of Chapter IV of Volume I of the Penal Code is the following Article 52 bis:

Article 52 bis

Anyone perpetrating a crime characterized as terrorist shall be punished by the sentence prescribed for the same crime not to be commuted to less than half the sentence.

Is characterized as terrorist any crime which involves an individual or collective project to cause harm to people or property with the aim of sowing terror and intimidation.

Shall be treated as crimes characterized as terrorist any acts advocating hatred, or racial or religious fanaticism whatever the means used.

For terrorist crimes, administrative control is mandatory for five years, sentences shall not be combined, and the provisions of Article 134 of this Law are applicable.

This Law shall be published in the Official Gazette of the Republic of Tunisia and shall be enforced as a law of the land.

Tunis, Date: November 22, 1993.

Zine el Abidine Ben Ali

---

(1) Preliminary proceedings. Deliberations of, and adoption by, the Chamber of Deputies during its session of November 16, 1993.

Law No. 113 of 1993, dated November 22, 1993, as an Amendment and Supplement to Certain Articles of the Code of Penal Procedures (1).

On behalf of the people,
After the approval of the Chamber of Deputies,
The President of the Republic proclaims the following law:

Article 1
Article 203 of the Code of Penal Procedures is hereby abrogated and substituted as follows: **Article 203 (New)**
Petition for a fine with regard to an infraction may not be lodged with a District Court if the fine requested exceeds the amount admissible in civil cases.

Article 2
Appended to Article 305 of the Code of Penal Procedures is the following paragraph:

Article 305 (New paragraph)
Tunisians may be prosecuted and tried by Tunisian courts if on foreign soil they commit one of the crimes referred to in Article 52 bis of the Penal Code, even when the aforementioned crimes are not recognizable crimes under the law of the country where they were perpetrated.

Article 3
Appended to the Code of Penal Procedures is the following new Article:

Article 307 bis (New)
Anyone who on foreign soil, as the first perpetrator or as an accomplice, commits a felony or a misdemeanor may be prosecuted and tried by Tunisian courts if the victim has Tunisian nationality. Prosecution shall be instigated only at the behest of the Public Prosecution following a complaint from the victim or his heirs.
Prosecution may not be instigated so long as the defendant proves that he has received a definitive judgement abroad, and where he was convicted, that he has served his sentence, that it has lapsed, or that he has been pardoned.

Article 4
Article 313 of the Code of Penal Procedures is hereby abrogated and substituted as follows:

Article 313 (New)
Extradition may also not be granted:
First—Where the felony or misdemeanor has a political character or where it transpires that the extradition request had a political motive whereas an attack on the life of the President of the Republic, of a member of his family, or of a member of the government does not count as a political crime.
Shall not count as a political crime those crimes referred to in Article 52 bis of the Criminal Law, where political asylum may not be granted.
Second—Where the crime for which extradition is requested involves a failure to discharge a military duty.
This Law shall be published in the Official Gazette of the Republic of Tunisia and shall be enforced as a law of the land.
Tunis, Date : November 22, 1993.

Zine el Abidine Ben Ali

---

(1) Preliminary proceedings. Deliberations of, and adoption by, the Chamber of Deputies during its session of November 16, 1993.

Law No. 114 of 1993, dated November 22, 1993, as an Amendment and Supplement to Certain Articles of the Code of Penal Procedures (1).

On behalf of the people,

After the approval of the Chamber of Deputies,

The President of the Republic proclaims the following law:

Article 1

Articles 85, 86 (the last paragraph), 87, 106, 107, 111 (the last paragraph), 205, 208, and 222 of the Code of Penal Procedures are hereby abrogated and substituted by the following provisions:

Article 85 (New)

A suspect may be remanded in custody in flagrante delicto felonies and misdemeanors as well as in the event of compelling evidence coming to light calling for remand as a security measure to prevent new crimes being committed, to ensure the sentence being served, or to guarantee the due process of the investigation.

Custody for the cases specified in the preceding paragraph may not exceed a period of six months. Where the interest of the investigation calls for the suspect to be remanded in custody the examining magistrate may, after consultation with the Public Prosecutor and by means of a corroborated decision, extend the custody period for a felony once only by no more than three months, and for a misdemeanor twice, on each occasion by no more than four months.

The said decision to extend custody is subject to appeal.

Release of the suspect is mandatory with or without bail after five days of interrogation where he has a specific place of residence and has not been previously sentenced to more than three months of imprisonment and where the legally prescribed sentence does not exceed one year of imprisonment.

---

(1) Preliminary proceedings. Deliberations of, and adoption by, the Chamber of Deputies during its session of November 16, 1993.

Some Provisions of the Penal Code
On the Incrimination of Hatred and Fanaticism

On that basis, the UN Working Group concluded that the proven acts of Ahmed Kahlaoui amount to incitement to racial hatred and constitute a crime, not an expression of opinion, and that therefore his arrest was not arbitrary.

On February 9, 1994, the Court of First Instance also sentenced one Nejib Al Baccouchi for similar offences. In a leaflet which he had written and distributed, entitled "Down with the Ben Yahia-Peres Agreement," he says, "The foul Jews have declared themselves the enemy. They bring treachery and treason...They spread AIDS, drugs, and spies...They forge currencies and pillage agriculture...So, what peace, what tolerance, what understanding are they brokering with the Jews...?"

On March 30, 1995, a third person by the name of Sami ben Hassine was convicted of similar offenses, and every time, Tunisia is showered with a flood of faxes and communications from human rights organizations demanding the release of such people on the grounds that they are prisoners of conscience.

On November 21, 1994, Tunisia took advantage of the United Nations Conference on Organized Crime in Naples, Italy, to put forward a proposal to treat extremist, terrorist crimes as crimes organized trans-nationally on a par with drug trafficking, arms dealing, trading in human organs, and environmental crimes, impelled by her conviction that fundamentalist extremism organizes itself across national boundaries: attacks are masterminded in one country, funds raised in another, and operatives recruited from a third to strike at varying targets.

During the April, 1995, Ninth United Nations Conference on the Prevention of Crime in Cairo, Tunisia moved beyond that proposal, dropping the term "terrorism" with its sensitive, controversial connotations in favor of the terms "fanaticism and hatred" to refer to extremist crimes, which she considered as serious crimes against humanity that should be prosecuted and severely sanctioned and should rally to the challenge international co-operation, at least with mandatory extradition and non-conferment of political asylum. The proposal was to face difficulties and eventual rejection, not least because several countries had already committed themselves to asylum for extremist figures on their territories, whom they were reluctant to extradite. Egypt then took on the submission of a draft proposal identical with the Tunisian Naples proposal, which was adopted by the Conference.[77] What is happening in the United Nations bespeaks the rapidly-changing international attitude toward extremism and growing awareness of its threat, as well as Tunisia's far-sighted commitment to new ways of containing this phenomenon by bolstering up international co-operation to find sound legal grounds that can deter such crimes to the satisfaction of democratic public opinion.

Besides the judicial apparatus, the media had a valuable part to play in the initial campaign for pluralism. The media may well be criticized for not keeping up to date with the Change, but that criticism applies least of all to the initial period when it stood in the firing line of the battle against fundamentalism as it took part in the anti-extremism awareness campaign. Had the media not been what it was at that time, the Change could not have occurred with the desired speed, and potential slips might well have been made, as, infiltrated by fundamentalists, and at times not awake to the threat to society, journalists

57

themselves could well rush to the support of extremism in the name of freedom of expression, out of sympathy, or after sensational news.

The media itself was not exempted from legal provisions to cover crimes of incitement to fanaticism and advocacy of hatred. On August 2, 1993, the Code of the Press was amended, with Article 44 now stating, "A prison term of two months to three years and a fine of one thousand to two thousand dinars is the penalty for anyone directly advocating by the means defined in Article 42 hatred between races, religions, or inhabitants, propagating ideas based on racial discrimination, religious extremism, instigating the offenses defined by Article 48, or urging the population to transgress the laws of the country," This amendment affecting the media illustrates once again the consistency of the plan to contain extremism.

Countless campaigns were organized against manifestations of extremism and fanaticism in the different media, which are worthy of in-depth studies that should highlight the new slogans and concepts devised to command people's attention and mobilize national public opinion.

The campaigns involved not only the government and the majority party press, but also all the national press, including that of the opposition. A new media discourse was born, and with the aid of the printed word or picture, it got to work, reporting, detailing, and reviewing crimes by these groups, providing historical pointers, comparing, cautioning.

The most poignant media action was perhaps the coverage of the Bab Souika incident on television, when Tunisians experienced closely, on February 18, 1991, the horror of what fanaticism may lead to. They were confronted with TV pictures of the innocent guards of one party headquarters, who had been hand-cuffed while extremists poured gasoline on them, and burned them to death. The masked group, wielding knives, had taken them by surprise in the early hours of that Sunday morning. Earlier, there also had been a TV screening of cit-izens who had been disfigured with acid, just for daring, in defiance of the wish-es of the extremist elements, to continue cautioning people against them. One of those disfigured was the Imam of a mosque, who later died. His only offense was that he had led people in prayer and preached to them. They considered him incapable of understanding Islam and so he had to be silent or be silenced.

In addition to the media, the political parties played their fair share in the mobilization of public opinion, leading thousands of public meetings under the banner either of the Democratic Constitutional Rally or of the democratic oppo-sition parties. The various party structures helped denounce extremist acts, awaken the sense of patriotism, and warn Tunisians against being ensnared into the traps and double talk of extremists. And Tunisians on their part, without exception, in my honest estimation, from all parts of the country and all walks of life, did not fail to be there in more than one meeting, eager and able to make their own contributions to the debate.

The political parties showed keen awareness, for they were the driving force behind civil society that other developing democracies could not muster, so thwarted were they in reaching a comprehensive alliance against fundamentalism by inter-party bickering that only ended where its threat began. And however often some used to state that the dangers besetting democracy, despite their seriousness, should not impede more freedoms and free competition, that amounted to no more than political tactics on their part, so parties there could keep up their line of opposition to and criticism of the ruling party.

Professional associations also had a vital part to play in preparing the socio-psychological ground for a liberal economic policy. This period was marked by dialogue and understanding between the government and professional associations of both employers and employees under the banner of independence with co-operation. As a matter of fact, a contractual policy was implemented within the context of a Framework Agreement initiated on April 17, 1990. The Tunisian National Trade Union in its Sousse Conference of April 20, 1989, carried out a bold purge of its structures, in response to the National Pact, which it had co-signed in order to align itself with the new government economic directions and uphold the political choice of democratic pluralism. The Tunisian Union of Industry and Commerce also effectively helped the state contain the social repercussions of liberal policies by a vigorous contribution to the national solidarity action. Moreover, it participated in funding political and cultural activities designed to instill the values of social harmony and marginalize fanaticism and extremism. An identical part was played by the National Farmers' Union. Businessmen, too, realized that the bedrock of development is political before being economical, and that confidence in the government and safety in society are the two essential incentives for more national and international investments as well as for greater enterprise and profit.

In addition, the professional associations now based their relationships on partnership, turning the page of discord that had so marked social life for some period of time.

What is notable is that the government did not sway to the left,[78] and managed to steer clear of the pitfalls that Tunisia along with several other countries of the region had previously slipped into. Earlier, in the 1970s, key government figures had supported the ideology of fundamentalism to win it over as an ally in blocking the advance of the left,[79] leading the whole government to fall into the trap and enabling fundamentalism in just a few years to work its way into security systems, into cultural and educational institutions, into associations, and into other structures.

That is why the new regime decided against such tactics, disdainful of setting leftism against fundamentalism and electing instead to establish common, middle-of-the road standards, which it set down in the National Pact. For this reason, we notice, the Tunisian Communist Workers' Party, well-known for its historical enmity for fundamentalism, was refused recognition, as its own principles and methods simply failed to meet the standards that Tunisia had set for itself.

For that party holds not with the principles of democratic pluralism, but with class conflict as a strategy to establish the rule of the proletariat and turn state power against capitalism. We will see elsewhere how reforms in the educational curricula brewed up a quiet battle to purge it of the clutches of fundamentalism while keeping it free of the fetters of leftism, as former officials in the Ministry of Education had wanted.

In the throes of confrontation, associations were given assistance to assume their part in combating fundamentalism. On August 2, 1988, the law on associations was amended to make their creation subject to authorization instead of prior permission. On April 2, 1992, new legislation was introduced to give citizens greater democratic practice and participation in the life of associations and to enable associations of a public character to carry out their civic mission within bounds neutral with regard to party politics and away from any political maneuvers.

The law guarantees the independence and political neutrality of associations by prohibiting anyone from concurrently holding key posts in a political party and in a public association. Today, Tunisia boasts more than 5200 associations, 2500 of which are active; 495 were set up in 1989, and 850 in 1990 and 1991. Boosting the number of associations created is part of the country's endeavor to establish democracy and fortify civil society.

The battle was taken right into the colleges and universities, which were not spared a confrontation. That confrontation was neither circumstantial, nor the work of individuals called upon by the President to serve in the education sector, for, as Secretary of State for Education at the time of the reform process, I had personal experience of Ben Ali's action plan as well as his scrupulous follow-up of its most minute details.

In his keynote speech of July 10, 1989, he explained his reasons for giving educational reform top priority. He had "entrusted the competent authorities, teachers and experts," he said, "with the mission of managing the affairs of the educational apparatus so as to pull it out of the quagmire it had sunk into because of successive fluctuating and inconsistent policies that stopped it coming up to the high expectations pinned on it." "Following consultations with the various scientific, social, and political bodies," he added, "it has become abundantly clear that we have to move beyond *ad hoc*, partial reforms to a radical change of our educational system, to build it upon new foundations that meet all the requirements, cultural and economic, of the new era of our history."

Ben Ali places education in "the vanguard of a civilizational change." As he states, in his speech of July 12, 1990, "A system that claims to be modern starts to be so only when its educational institutions are able to assume a vanguard position in spreading among people, and particularly our little ones, such a sound knowledge, such a deep, objective understanding of the harsh reality of life as to instill in them an awareness of the essential values to a human society that are the bedrock of a civic life and the springboards for uninhibited creativity and initiative, namely the respect of human beings and human rights."

Schools in particular received personal attention from the President, who worked hard to carry out a meticulous review and follow-up of the curricula that purges it of texts or references advocating the cause of fanaticism. That is because fundamentalist figures in education had been taking advantage, since the early 1970s, of the cover and backing they received under the pretext of fighting the left.

Insidiously they had slithered into the system, preaching their doctrine and rhetoric to young children in the early stages of learning, or in subsequent academic years through insinuations of their political ideology in carefully selected language, history, philosophy, and other texts propagating their particular brand of Islam. What they had in mind was to raise children in hatred and the declaring heretical of other civilizations, since Islam, in their opinion, preaches one exclusive civilization. They wanted to inculcate a fundamentalist ideology that puts in clear relief what they believe to be the true Islam while relegating other societies to a heretical status. They went so far as to defend the beating of women, justifying slavery, and declaring unbelievers all those who would not conform to their rituals. Those and other equally peculiar ideas are their stock-in-trade, which Tunisia, within an integrated plan, waged a long drawn-out, arduous battle to uproot from school curricula. Thus, the new regime took it upon itself to designate several committees[80] to supplant the antiquated with new values of patriotism, openness to other cultures, tolerance, equality of men and women, cohesion of the family, partnership, a work ethic, the love of freedom and of one's neighbor, an appreciation of citizenship, human solidarity, and a host of other values that break irretrievably with the teachings of the past.

Tunisia's most significant decision has been to eschew the past error of politicizing educational curricula. She simply refused to allow fundamentalism to take hold in the minds of the young, and refused to let leftism take its place. Instead, she elected for the curricula to foster a sound environment based on citizenship, patriotism, and a revived human spirit. Ben Ali was unequivocal from the start, referring to those who would seize the opportunity to reinstate leftism through the educational backdoor.

On July 17, 1991, Science Day, he reminded officials that the basic aim of the reform was "to raise the young generations on unswerving loyalty to Tunisia in repayment of her rightful claims upon us all, that we might proclaim: let there be none in our midst who would not settle in their own identity, who would change their skin (an obvious enough reference), for ours is a generous land steeped in a history which, by dint of heroic feats and triumphs, of supreme sacrifices, of an unrelenting struggle for freedom, of a burning ambition to keep abreast of modern civilization, and of enduring battles and challenges, has enabled our Arab Islamic civilization to storm inexorably ahead on ennobling causes, to bring enlightenment to humanity in its darkest ages, and to grow increasingly enriched, nay, fertilized by an open contact with the other without having to relinquish its own identity."

The reform of the educational material and curricula was coupled with an upgrading of the teaching staff. Teachers and headmasters who were members of the extremist movement were expelled. Otherwise teachers were able to get on refresher courses or retrain to better serve the new orientations, since education is an area with a direct bearing on politics that Ben Ali regards as strategic in every sense of the word: A quarter of the population are children and young people at school, one-third of those in employment work in education, and one-fourth of government expenditure is spent on this sector.[81]

Colleges and universities too underwent and participated in a screening process, which they had awaited for years. Teachers who were members of the fundamentalist movement were investigated and the Tunisian National Students' Union, the student wing of the *Nahdha* movement and the conveyor feeding it not only its leaders but its criminal action operatives as well, was dissolved. (The paradox of a graduate exploding bombs, by the way, is a mystery that can only be resolved in the light of the dogmatic character of such organizations.) Neutrality was finally made possible for the university, with protection given to the silent majority, which had lived in fear of the terrorism practiced by the fanatic students. Since 1988, the rate of strikes has been on the decline, and from the beginning of 1992, the silent majority imposed itself, with the university now able to lead a normal life and lectures taking place regularly. A dramatic increase was brought about in student entertainment and leisure activities in a bid to occupy students' spare time, which had earlier been left idle.

Political discourse inside the university underwent a change too, no longer a discourse of objection but of participation. The colleges and universities, previously aloof and isolated, now became open, engaged in co-operation with ambient institutions, and connected with their political presence, with participation from teachers and students in the formulation and implementation of national policies.

That is the scope of the multilateral action. That action involved not only security, the judiciary, the media, and education, but also Tunisian diplomacy, which had been facing such external pressure in the name of human rights and the right of fundamentalists to co-exist as tested the conduct of its awareness campaigns. Its mission was only eased as of the beginning of 1992, when the West realized the dangers of these movements and their activities on its territories, not least of which was the damage to its investment and trade interests. The Gulf countries too realized those same dangers.

The multilateral action also involved the cultural institutions, which unleashed humor and wit to tackle the threat of extremism and expose its double standards. There was especially the making of such famous films as *Riyh as-Sadd* and *Halfaouine*, which deride those who hide behind religion, putting on a pious appearance to the outside world, only to engage secretly in debauchery and sin. Cultural associations were also born that grouped distinguished national elites, who deployed their own perspective to address extremism in a widely popular style, such as the Journalists' Club (May, 1992), the Book Center (April, 1993), the Poets' Society (November, 1993), and so on and so forth.

The most vital action, however, was that affecting socio-economic life. Ben Ali had already made his views known on the matter. There was to be no genuine freedom without development. Likewise, development could not be durable without freedom. The two were correlative elements, neither a prerequisite for the other. Therefore the existence of democracy depended on the existence of an adequate human environment, adequate employment and living standards.[82] So, unfaltering and unequivocal, he decided on a liberal economy, now to open up to the external world, tap the private sector's capacity for enterprise and initiative, and fire Tunisia's individual potential for development.[83] Radical reforms were introduced that liberated imports, prices, and investments, reduced tariffs, and fortified the stock exchange. Another significant reform was made in the area of taxation to streamline, make transparent, and reduce rates. Additional reforms are currently underway in the areas of education and vocational training to ensure such flexibility as meets the needs of a growing economy in terms of employment and skilled work force.[84] In actual fact, many indicators do show that Tunisia is economically well-equipped for pluralism. Per capita income reached 1850 dinars in 1994, where it had been only one-fifth of that in 1960. The Gross National Product has been growing at a steady rate of 5% in recent years and inflation held in check at 4.7%. The balance of payments deficit was brought down to just 1.9% of the GNP, while savings were propped up to 24.6% of the GNP. Price de-control has attained 90% at the production stage and 50% at the distribution stage. Free imports have reached as much as 90%, while the maximum tariff stood at 43%. The private sector invests up to 63% in industry, soaring to 98% in tourism, for example.

Nevertheless, what has made Tunisia stand out is its ability to curb the negative repercussions of a free economy by implementing a prudent social policy of aid and relief. The government worked to launch social solidarity programs within the framework of the National Solidarity Fund, better known as the 2626 Account. This is an open-credit account for voluntary contributions earmarked for improving life in poor neighborhoods and remote areas, which Ben Ali refers to as "Shadow Zones." The aim of these programs is not just to procure the contributions, but also to create a social dynamism that precludes any feeling of marginalization on the part of the poor while stirring in the rich the sentiment that they are nationally accountable for social welfare, that their personal success and comfort are not the product of an individual but of a collective endeavor by the whole community.

We can thus appreciate the social dimension of Tunisia's political program, one facet of which is the President's own regular, TV-documented visits to poor neighborhoods and rural areas to see for himself people's living conditions and to do everything in his power to bring about tangible improvements, which the President closely monitors through media coverage and which have won him a special place in people's affection.

That grassroots interaction, while breaking with the red tape approaches of the past, was not achieved without generating belief and confidence in the government, bringing relief to the badly off, and prompting them to demand even more rights of local authorities and party structures. Additionally, parties and charitable associations spare no efforts in providing assistance to the needy on school entrance and other social and religious occasions.

Here, we need only adduce two token samples first presented by Taoufik Baccar in his lecture on "The Tunisian Model of Socio-Economic Development."[85] The first sample relates to the human development indicator, which the United Nations Development Program favors over per capita income as a more com-

Liberty of Human Development

Without liberty, human development is incomplete. Throughout history, individuals have sacrificed their lives to gain access to national and personal liberty. Very recently, we have witnessed the huge wave of liberty which has swept Eastern Europe, South Africa, and numerous other parts of the world. A human development indicator must then give sufficient weight to the liberty that a society enjoys in the pursuit of its material and social objectives. The value which we place on comparable achievements in different countries varies according to whether these have been accomplished within a democratic or an authoritarian framework.

Whereas it is necessary to establish a qualitative judgement, no simple quantifiable measure currently covers the many aspects of human liberty—free elections, multiparty politics, uncensored press, adherence to the rule of the law, freedom of expression, etc. To a certain extent, however, the composite Human Development Indicator (HDI) captures a few aspects of human liberty.

For example, if repression annihilates the creativity and productivity of individuals, this will show up in income estimates or in levels of illiteracy. Moreover, the concept of human development adopted in this Report centers around the capacities of individuals, that is to say, their ability to manage their own affairs—which, after all, is the essence of liberty.

The table below presents a selection of countries (in each region of the world) which have attained a high level of human development (compared to other countries of the region) within a reasonably democratic political and social framework. A superficial examination of the ranking of the countries given in Table 1 on Human Development Indicators, at the end of this report, reveals that the countries who DHI is high are also equipped with a democratic framework, with hardly any exception.

A great deal of empirical work must be done to quantify the diverse indicators of human liberty and to perform a more thorough analysis of the existing link between it and human development. The top-ranking 15 countries in the area of democratic human development:

Country	HDI	Country	HDI
Latin America and Caribbean		**Middle East and North Africa**	
Costa Rica	0,916	Turkey	0,751
Uruguay	0,916	**Tunisia**	**0,657**
Trinidad and Tobago	0,885		
Mexico	0,876	**Sub-Saharan Africa**	
Venezuela	0,861	Mauritius	0,788
Jamaica	0,824	Botswana	0,646
Colombia	0,801	Zimbabwe	0,576
Asia			
Malaysia	0,800		
Sri Lanka	0,789		
Thailand	0,783		

United Nations Development Program
Report on Human Development 1990

UNDP 1995

Evolution of Human Development Indicator (HDI) in time: Ranking and Values for 1970 and 1992

		Value of HDI 1970	1992	Value Evol. in%	Rank in '70 -Rank in '92			Value of HDI 1970	1992	Value Evol in%	Rank in '70 -Rank in '92
1	Sweden	0,764	0,919	20	2	41	Sri Lanka	0,468	0,660	41	−7
2	Finland	0,714	0,918	29	6	**42**	**Tunisia**	**0,274**	**0,641**	**135**	**16**
3	Norway	0,719	0,911	27	4	43	Ecuador	0,425	0,641	51	−4
4	Denmark	0,759	0,904	19	0	44	Peru	0,423	0,631	49	−4
5	United States	0,810	0,901	11	−4	45	Paraguay	0,475	0,628	32	−12
6	Australia	0,725	0,901	24	0	46	Philippines	0,455	0,625	37	−9
7	France	0,742	0,898	21	−2	47	Iran, Islamic Rep. of	0,301	0,611	103	9
8	Japan	0,702	0,896	28	2	48	Indonesia	0,307	0,591	92	5
9	Canada	0,766	0,891	16	−7	49	Dominican Republic	0,407	0,590	45	−6
10	Austria	0,685	0,882	29	4	50	Guyana	0,490	0,584	19	−20
11	Barbados	0,595	0,878	48	9	51	Arab Rep. of Syria	0,306	0,571	87	3
12	New Zealand	0,691	0,868	26	0	52	Nicaragua	0,369	0,560	52	−5
13	United Kingdom	0,690	0,862	25	0	53	El Salvador	0,384	0,533	39	−9
14	Italy	0,651	0,861	32	2	54	Honduras	0,343	0,524	53	−5
15	Belgium	0,696	0,852	22	−4	55	Iraq	0,263	0,523	99	5
16	Netherlands	0,702	0,851	21	−7	56	Saudi Arabia	0,242	0,514	113	10
17	Portugal	0,502	0,832	66	12	57	Swaziland	0,261	0,508	94	4
18	Greece	0,570	0,825	45	4	58	Algeria	0,252	0,508	101	6
19	Singapore	0,519	0,822	58	7	59	Papua New Guinea	0,269	0,487	81	0
20	Ireland	0,618	0,813	32	−3	60	Guatemala	0,309	0,481	56	−8
21	Thailand	0,448	0,798	78	17	61	Lesotho	0,322	0,466	45	−10
22	Spain	0,600	0,795	32	−4	62	Ghana	0,259	0,460	78	1
23	Luxembourg	0,674	0,790	17	−8	63	Egypt	0,261	0,453	74	−1
24	Trinidad and Tobago	0,555	0,786	42	−1	64	Morocco	0,223	0,450	102	3
25	Malaysia	0,422	0,768	82	16	65	Myanmar	0,339	0,448	32	−15
26	Argentina	0,580	0,768	32	−5	66	Zambia	0,291	0,403	38	−9
27	Venezuela	0,515	0,765	48	0	67	India	0,250	0,401	60	−2
28	Panama	0,504	0,765	52	0	68	Togo	0,186	0,380	105	4
29	Costa Rica	0,533	0,763	43	−4	69	Pakistan	0,196	0,360	84	1
30	Chile	0,543	0,759	40	−6	70	Tanzania, United Rep. of	0,197	0,359	82	−1
31	Turkey	0,381	0,744	95	15	71	Haiti	0,209	0,354	69	−3
32	Mexico	0,476	0,741	56	−1	72	Bangladesh	0,174	0,334	92	1
33	Fiji	0,467	0,722	55	2	73	Sudan	0,189	0,332	76	−2
34	Colombia	0,460	0,720	56	2	74	Malawi	0,157	0,315	100	0
35	Kuwait	0,475	0,716	51	−3	75	Nepal	0,128	0,310	143	1
36	Jamaica	0,598	0,710	19	−175	76	Mozambique	0,150	0,229	52	−1
37	Brazil	0,418	0,709	69	17	77	Ethiopia	0,106	0,217	105	1
38	Botswana	0,302	0,696	131	6	78	Guinea	0,110	0,214	96	−1
39	Bahrain	0,383	0,686	79	8	79	Afghanistan	0,084	0,169	101	0
40	United Arab Emirates	0,352	0,674	92							

United Nations Development Program
Report on Human Development 1995

prehensive indicator, integrating quantitative development as related to qualitative human development.

More precisely, it is calculated on the basis of living standards, life expectancy at birth, and educational level. The 1994 United Nations Development Program Report, referring to Tunisia, had this to say: "It has given top priority in the use of its resources to improving living standards, thereby striking a balance between the requirements of development and the social dimension."

That balance, called by Dr. John Badge "Shared Development," has been a difficult one to achieve for many other developing countries, since the same report shows Tunisia ranked 81st on the basis of human development and only 85th on the basis of per capita income, a positive difference of plus four points. That situation is precisely the reverse for many other countries.

In the 1995 Report Tunisia improved its ranking to 75th. However, if we take into account equality of men and women, Tunisia leaps to 59th out of 130 countries.

The second sample relates to Tunisia's credibility in world financial circles, with the competent agencies awarding Tunisia a useful risk-factor rating (3b positive) that has allowed her to secure from world markets financial facilities on satisfactory conditions.

Nowhere has that been more evident as when Tunisia managed to secure from Japan's International Stock Exchange (The Samurai) a loan to the tune of 300 million dollars with an interest rate of not more than 5.85%, including a 1.6% bank margin. Compared to arrangements in force in this Exchange, those are indeed very favorable terms.

Tawfik Baccar goes on to compare the Pre- and Post-Change Eras. By 1987, an adverse evolution of the foreign factor had crippled Tunisia's ability to resist foreign fluctuations, its adopted economic model no longer coping with the new realities.

In the mid-'80s the economic outlook had become intolerably bleak, what with a deteriorating development level, poor job creation records, and a total collapse of both domestic and foreign financial balances, with borrowing levels and debt services climbing to 60% and 28% respectively, and the Government Budget Deficit and the Balance of Payments Deficit reaching, respectively, 5.5% and 8% of the Gross National Product.

And despite significant wage increases, the social policy intended to succeed at the expense of economic viability soon cracked at the seams, fomenting social tensions once again, which now urgently called for the necessary economic reviews and reforms to be undertaken.

The speaker then describes how the first stage of a rescue mission was started in 1986 with emergency measures to secure the major financial balances. In fact, a restructuring reform program had been launched within the Seventh Plan, 1987-1991. Nevertheless, that economic reform suffered the lack of a national consensus compounded with the absence of a social environment of trust and confidence, all running in short supply at that time.

The country was now ripe for a solution to the political crisis as the key to the way out of the socio-economic impasse it had been collared into. That solution came in the guise of the November 1987 Change.

To apply a socio-economic remedy is to dry out the roots of extremism and sanitize the festering soil it thrives on to pick its recruits.

Thus Tunisia has managed to turn the conflict with extremism around from one directed against the state into a social concern, implicating the whole community. Parties and associations, elites and grassroots have all charged to the fray in the belief that the eradication of extremism is no longer the exclusive preserve of one political party or of one social group. Rather, it is the common denominator that has rallied all Tunisians to ban violence and fanaticism.

As discussed below, the National Pact, Tunisia's national statement of guidelines for political activity, has been the catalyst that unifies Tunisians around that one orientation and discourse.[86] As the Tunisian saying goes, Tunisians today have been doubly immunized: first against socialism, following the fiasco of the Cooperative Policy in the '60s, and second against fundamentalism, following the policies exposing and unmasking it in the '90s.

That is the first challenge to secure the transition to pluralism: overflow control and the prevention of bubbles and bursts. The second challenge is internal to the regime. It lay in the redistribution of power and the creation of the institutions that are to prepare the ground for pluralism and break with the unilateral mentality. □

THE SECOND CHALLENGE:
The Redistribution of Power

THE NOVEMBER 7TH CHANGE breathed new life at once in the government and in the political parties, as Ben Ali moved to redistribute political power and strengthen its ability to attain the new objectives of the Change: political competition, a free economy, and a balanced, open, tolerant society. While, to the regime, political and social overflow control was an external challenge, the redistribution of power was an internal one, both crucial and sensitive.

Ben Ali assumed control of a dying regime, which had been reduced to rival factions feuding over succession to a man who had so aged as to lose his grip on things. Habib Bourguiba, one of the leaders of the liberation movement and an impassioned patriot, had been able, certainly not unaided by fellow activists, to lead Tunisia to independence, to give her what no other president could have given her, a drive for modernization, particularly with the liberation of women and the introduction of universal education, while steering clear of the nationalistic trends that were the order of the day in most Arab regimes of that time.[87]

Ironically, what Bourguiba did for the country turned out to be its undoing. He liberated the country, not the individual human being, and created institutions devoid of life or spirit. Superimposed structures, they were propped up with no firm foundation in public conviction or in popular participation. He founded the state apparatus, but in the declining years of his presidency, he monopolized power, turning administration into a bureaucratic, personal instrument that gradually became estranged from people and their aspirations and ended up in isolation. Freedom was gone and the spirit of political competitiveness was thin on the ground. But what had exacerbated matters was the economic centralization and continuous intervention of the state in all production and marketing sectors, turning the state itself into a huge machinery incapable of motivation, sharing, or mobilization.

The remoteness of the state from people's regenerating aspirations escalated the crisis and fueled popular feeling into pent-up anger. That pushed the state to resort to its repressive forces to impose its will and secure domestic peace, thus failing to find an adequate and flexible solution to take in the new inputs, and to meet popular demands while channeling them to serve its basic priorities. Hence, the recurrent crises of 1969, when the Co-operative Policy caused popular anger to erupt, of 1978 with the Trade Union crisis, and of 1984 with the so-called Bread Riots. Each time the regime managed to restore order, only to brace itself for the postponed, but even more critical crisis to come.[88]

It is that suffocation of the regime before 1987 which prompted Ben Ali, then Prime Minister, to forestall the next crisis, which surely would have been explosive. He moved simply to carry out the constitutional duty prescribed in such cases and assumed the presidency, after a medical committee had declared Bourguiba unfit to continue in office.

From that time on, the new regime embarked upon a new course. Determined to avoid the errors of the past, it had learned the basic lessons for the future: to banish the personality cult and work within the law, through institutions, popular participation in decision-making, and the institution of competition as the instrument for selection of the fittest, whether in politics or in the economy, provided these steps are gradually introduced, not dropped precipitately upon a society whose capacity to generate demands, at least initially, is far in excess of its capacity to absorb, or take in, the actual realization of those demands.

To compare Ben Ali's approach to government with that of Bourguiba, one could say, at the risk of oversimplification, that while Bourguiba was essentially interested in the state, Ben Ali has also been eager to invest in society; while Bourguiba banked on liberating the country, Ben Ali has banked on liberating the individual human being. As Bourguiba's style grew more authoritarian and patriarchal, Ben Ali's grew more understanding of the changes afoot. His statement on Change Day drives that point home: "Our people have reached such a degree of awareness and maturity that all our sons and daughters, all the different sectors, can now make a constructive contribution to the running of their affairs."

Suffice it to mention here the most important reforms, which all relate to a redistribution of power in a broad sense: the abolition of the presidency for life, the revival of Parliament, the rehabilitation of the judiciary, the reinforcement of constitutional and administrative audits and controls, the redefinition of the role of the ruling party, empowering associations to take part in discharging national responsibilities, giving the elites a say in decision-making, and more generally the dissemination of a new political culture that reflects the mood of the new regime.

No to the Presidency for Life

As early as his declaration on Change Day, November 7, 1987, Ben Ali put an end to the presidency for life. Hard on the heels of that decision there came an amendment of the constitution, dated July 25, 1988, a date which he chose to coincide with Tunisia's yearly Republic Day. The Presidency was now made subject to regular elections every five years that restored to the Republican Regime its true meaning.

Analysts today overlook that amendment, as if it could be taken for granted, while in point of fact it was a far-reaching move with even more far-reaching consequences that repudiated the personality cult and did away with the clinging attitude to power. The President of the Republic is now subject to the ballot-box, as every five years he submits to a public referendum and has to abide by people's choice. At the same time, he is obliged to keep a regular interface and dialogue with the people, attend to their demands, and continually seek their confidence. One need only note the sheer contrast between Bourguiba's attitude toward the people and that of Ben Ali. Where the former stood ever indifferent, and even haughty, the latter exudes enthusiasm for dialogue and closeness.

The presidency for life not only affected the conduct of the President, but also of his advisers and opponents. For as the previous era was marred by a conflict that had boiled down to a squabble over succession as all awaited the death of the man in power, reduced to flattery, dissimulation, and waiting about, the new era has been marked by a conflict of ideas and programs, as all vie to excel, advisers to win the trust of the President and opponents to win the trust of the people.[89]

A Fresh Start for Parliament

The Change gave Parliament a fresh start and restored to it the distinction of authority.[90]

The admission of opposition parties into Parliament as well as the few seats they have obtained highlights the change. Their presence, though standing at just 19 representatives, has transformed the plenary sessions. The 19 members represent four parties out of the six legally recognized parties that took part in the elections of March 20, 1994, and cover the ideological spectrum: leftists, nationalists, and socialists. Their contributions are valued by public opinion and the media for shedding new light upon proposed legislation. The deliberations on new legislation are an opportunity to lay on the table all the current points of contention between the political parties, reflecting the actual competing ideological persuasions of the different social groups. The Parliamentary deliberations, whether on legislative proposals or on the budget, are an occasion, the observer will note, for the opposition representatives to address not so much the House as the printed media and TV for as wide a broadcasting as possible of their ideas and proposals. And while they may not be able today to affect the majority, they are still able to influence public opinion as they prepare for a more effective political presence.

The new impetus affected not only the opposition parties, but also the representatives of the majority party, the Democratic Constitutional Rally (RCD), which, in many respects, has been stimulated by the presence of the opposition itself. To start with, attendance of the plenary sessions has swelled, with a very low rate of absenteeism. Preparations to speak for government-sponsored projects, which undergo a meticulous individual or group examination before submission, are now better and more thorough. For more important legislation, preparatory meetings are held at the RCD Central Office, the main headquarters of the majority party representatives, whose conception of legislation is no longer purely technical, but also politically relevant, and whose style has acquired more sensitivity to the dispositions of public opinion, and more of the clarity and prudence demanded of broadcast statements.

The entry of opposition into Parliament, Ben Ali believes, serves not only the opposition itself, but the ruling party too, inspiring it with renewed discipline and vigor. What's more, an inevitable benefit accrues to the whole of society, with the stimulation of a national dialogue on the various issues which accompany the proposal of bills, the discussion of the budget, as well as government question-time sessions.

A pluralist Parliament has also had an impact on the government's own work. Its perspective of legislation is now more political, for tabling a proposal now requires of government members greater efforts to win over public opinion. And the technical preparation of a bill now proceeds hand in hand with the preparation for its media coverage, since it is not enough for the bill to be technically sound, viable, and effective; it has to be acceptable to public opinion, too.

Parliament enjoyed not only that new internal atmosphere, but also a new relationship to the executive branch. It was no longer to be viewed as a subordinate council, but now as a major constitutional power, on equal footing with the other powers. Since the Change, there has been a total compliance with the provisions of the Constitution with respect to the solid protection of the legislative terms of reference of Parliament as defined by the Constitution, as well as compliance with deadlines for the submission of proposals, and with rules of procedure for applications of extraordinary reviews. Many have been the cases too where the recommendations of Standing Committees have been adopted for amendments to the proposals before them, because of their serious-mindedness and in response to the wishes of the representatives of the people as well.

The representative council was helped in fully carrying out its duties, not least by the President of the Republic, who has demonstrated absolute compliance with the Constitution as well as respect for its institutions.

Unlike Bourguiba, who, by nature and because of his prolonged term at the head of the state, was set on usurping the role of institutions and personalizing power, in the belief that he owned the regime and held the secret to all important matters of state,[91] Ben Ali has been living by a different set of values, diametrically opposed to the first. He came to reform institutions and restore normality. Training and experience in senior government positions meant he remained constant to the law and traditions, committed to working within the framework of institutions.

The World Atlas of Risks

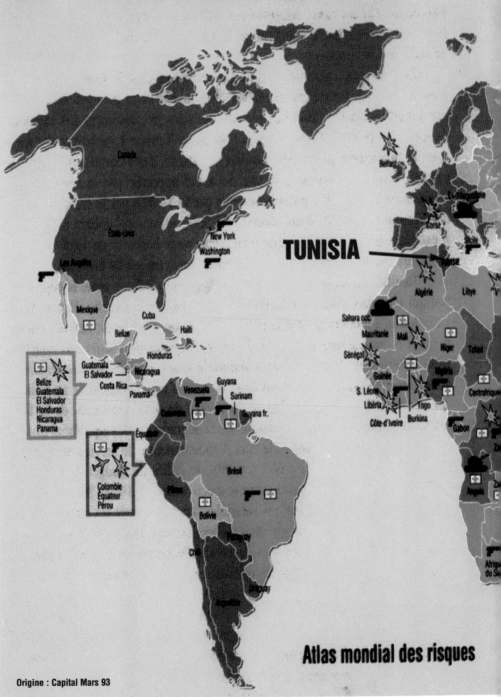

Canada

États-Unis

New York
Washington

Los Angeles

Mexique

Cuba

Belize

Haïti

Honduras

Guatemala
El Salvador   Nicaragua

Costa Rica

Panama

Belize
Guatemala
El Salvador
Honduras
Nicaragua
Panama

Colombie
Équateur
Pérou

Équateur

Venezuela

Guyana

Surinam

Guyana fr.

Colombie

Brésil

Pérou

Bolivie

Paraguay

Chili

Uruguay

Argentine

TUNISIA

Belfast

Ex-Yougoslavie

Tunisie

Algérie   Libye

Sahara occ.

Mauritanie   Mali

Niger   Tchad

Sénégal

Guinée

Nigéria

S. Léone

Centrafrique

Libéria

Togo

Côte-d'Ivoire   Burkina

Gabon

Angola

Afrique
du Sud

Atlas mondial des risques

Origine : Capital Mars 93

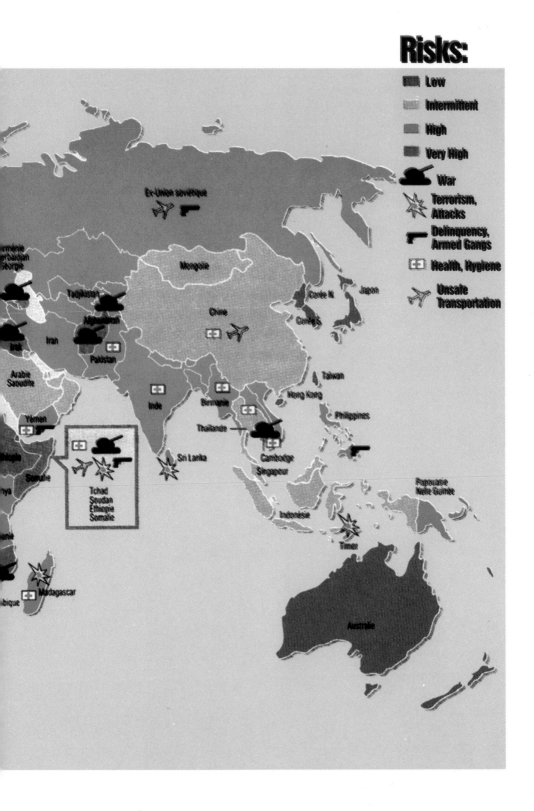

Risks:

Low

Intermittent

High

Very High

War

Terrorism, Attacks

Delinquency, Armed Gangs

Health, Hygiene

Unsafe Transportation

Ex-Union soviétique

Arménie
Azerbaïdjan
Géorgie

Tadjikistan

Afghanistan

Iran

Irak

Pakistan

Arabie
Saoudite

Yémen

Mongolie

Chine

Corée N.

Corée S.

Japon

Taiwan

Hong Kong

Inde

Birmanie

Thaïlande

Cambodge

Singapour

Philippines

Sri Lanka

Tchad
Soudan
Éthiopie
Somalie

Éthiopie

Somalie

Kenya

Mozambique

Madagascar

Papouasie
Nelle Guinée

Indonésie

Timor

Australie

That is why whoever comes to know Ben Ali closely cannot help feeling his highly developed sense of organization, his reverence of the law, his respect for institutions, and his adherence to etiquette and protocol.

The Return of the Third Power

Among the branches of government that had a robust comeback, after much marginalization and subordination, is the judiciary. Judges regained their full powers, answering to no one but the law. During a public political meeting in Bab Souika, one judge, I recall, who was a veteran of the liberation movement and had been a critic of Bourguiba during his rule, made a charming but constitutionally very perceptive and pertinent remark. He compared the state to the traditional coal stove used by Tunisians for cooking. The stove, like the state, stands not on two, but three feet, a simile that points to the importance of the judiciary to the regime's balance.

As noted earlier, on December 29, 1987, only days after the Change, the abolition of the State Security Court—which, not being composed exclusively of judges and not working by ordinary procedures, could not guarantee a fair trial—marked the end of the era of political trials. On that same date the State Prosecutor's office was abolished, an instrument of interference in the justice process that served to perpetrate bizarre abuses, many of them for political motives, but some for personal ones in ordinary civil cases.[92]

The Supreme Judicial Council has now recovered its full powers. Ben Ali himself is anxious to preside over its annual meetings. The Council passes in review the affairs of judges in terms of appointment, promotion, transfer, and discipline. Its proceedings are prepared by the Government's General Counselor, the Director of Judicial Affairs, who is now assisted, as of the 1993 Meeting, by a committee of five that emanates from the Council. These measures have been met with great relief from judges who see them as guarantees of fairness in their professional promotion and transfer.

The Tunisian Association of Judges, which is the trade union that defends their interests both judicially and administratively, is also back to its normal activities, following a strained period of marginalization. Three members of the former Executive Council of the Association of Young Judges, who had been convicted of approving a strike before the courts and consequently dismissed from their duties, have been granted an amnesty. The Association of Young Judges had emerged during the old regime as an alternative to the first fraternity, then regarded as pro-government. After the Change, the offshoot withered as the original association regained credibility. The three judges shortly resumed work with a retroactive confirmation of service for the dismissal period.

The Bar has remained independent, enjoying self-rule through a national union elected every three years. The union, which is the scene for intense competition acted out between the different ideological and political persuasions, is able to carry out its defense duties in unabridged autonomy and freedom from the government.

Yet on more than one occasion, the Dean of the National Bar Association has described how a newfound climate of cooperation with the authorities has allowed lawyers to operate more effectively without at any time depriving them of their customary independence.

What is more striking is how the independence enjoyed by the Tunisian Association of Judges and the National Bar Association in this era of the Change has prompted them to a jealous defense of the regime vis-à-vis foreign agencies, international forums, and non-governmental organizations, whenever they felt there was a political agenda to do damage to Tunisia's interests or to distort the facts of the matter on liberties or guarantees of a fair trial.[93]

Tunisia's judicial system, in contradistinction with that of similar countries, prides itself on many achievements. For a start, there is one judge to every 8,000 inhabitants, whereas in France, for instance, which has a similar system of justice, the ratio is one to every 10,000. Second, one-quarter of the judges are women, that is, around 260. Third, courts are distributed throughout the Republic, bringing judicial services within citizens' reach.

Also, as of May 17, 1993, the publication of lawsuits became free, as disputants were exempted from publication fees, which used to be paid before the start of the hearing and increased as the case went up the judicial hierarchy. As such the fees stood as a genuine stumbling-block to judicial equality.[94]

Moreover, having recourse to legal representation is no longer obligatory in labor suits, civil cases, and straightforward cases tried before Local Area Courts and involving sums of not more than 7000 dinars. Additionally, a legal advice scheme is available in primary courts completely free of charge. And each court has a permanent desk, offering legal services to all citizens outside office hours.

Court procedures guarantee a dual judicial hierarchy for hearings as well as the right of appeal to the Court of Cassation. Adjudication is made at the rate of 3.6 months in each hierarchical step. The rate of judgments appealed, standing at 27% for Appellate cases and 5% for Cassation cases, remains in line with acceptable norms and testifies to the satisfaction of litigants with the verdicts returned.

However, some of the most significant guarantees introduced in the penal domain are those we have alluded to in earlier paragraphs. They have to do with the protection of arrestees before trial by limiting the period of custody and making it subject to certain conditions monitored by a judge. Custody periods have in fact been reduced, with trial scheduling priority given to those under arrest.[95] Hard-labor sentences as well as rehabilitation service have been abolished too. A system for the automatic restitution of full rights has been installed to reinstate convicts unconditionally within a set period of time after the sentence is served or after an amnesty, without having to submit their case to a specialized committee.

Not least of all the changes is the new respect conferred upon judges as the judiciary has regained enhanced status within society. Following the Change, judges now receive the highest salary in the civil service, where it had been one of the lowest. By protocol, judges now command a distinguished position on formal occasions. The First President of the Court of Cassation, the dean of the courts, has now been promoted to the rank of Secretary of State. The profession is today in brisk demand, making judges justifiably proud.

The President of the Republic, who now attends the opening of the judicial session as the President of the Supreme Judicial Council, stands in salute as the judiciary enters the court, signaling his respect for the judicial institution and what it stands for, as well as a sharp contrast with the former President.

Repeatedly the course of events has demonstrated just how far the President respects the judiciary, and abides by the law and pronouncements of the courts. For instance, he has been reluctant to avail himself of his constitutional prerogatives of granting amnesty to a convict who had not served a minimum term of imprisonment, for no other reason than his worry, as he says, that his action might be interpreted as an act of defiance to the court, releasing a prisoner where it had ordered his incarceration. As a result, a high-profile figure had to serve a whole year of his term before obtaining a pardon, despite having the President's personal compassion as well as public sympathy, since he had not been a principal perpetrator but a passive accessory to a charge of misappropriation of public funds. What held the President back from issuing an immediate pardon after the verdict had been his respect for the judgment of the court.

There are two other incidents which I must develop with some detail. One evening, I received a phone call from the Public Prosecutor of a prosperous seacoast Governorate who informed me that a bailiff had been threatened with arrest if he tried again to enforce a ruling requiring a redefinition of the boundaries of the Governor's Official Residence grounds. The plaintiff, the Governor's neighbor, had been summoned to the Police Station to sign a deposition to the effect that he had instigated the enforcement procedure without the knowledge of the Governor. Accordingly, I raised the matter with the President, who was infuriated at the outrage and ordered that the decision be enforced, the bailiff and the plaintiff be called to receive the Public Prosecutor's apologies and assurances for being wronged, and that legal proceedings be instituted against those who had abused power. A few days later, the Governor was relieved of his duties.

In the second incident, I had been informed by the Public Prosecutor of a neighboring Governorate that a bailiff had been prevented from impounding trucks owned by a local industrial tycoon. In the middle of the enforcement procedure, he had received instructions from the Government's Local Commissioner ordering him to stop the operation and return matters to what they had been prior to his intervention. I informed the Minister of the Interior, who immediately spoke to the Governor on the subject. A few hours later, the bailiff was invited to complete his mission. I then informed the President, who expressed his stupefaction at such an abuse. Awhile later, the Governor was called to other duties.

It would be tedious to relate everything, but events I have personally experienced have convinced me of Ben Ali's deep conviction that interference in the judiciary jeopardizes the regime's balance, and that the autonomy and impartiality of the judge are two keystones in building the society of his vision.

Here, we need only give a brief account of how the outlawed organizations and the cases of hatred and fanaticism were tried before the courts. As discussed on previous pages, at no point was there recourse to extraordinary courts, as the cases were within the jurisdiction of the different courts of the Republic, according to territorial competence. Ordinary too were the procedures followed, in fact those same ones in force for all crimes. In attendance at the trials were a significant number of lawyers, who exercised full defense rights unimpeded, as well as observers from humanitarian organizations. Unlike other countries, at no time did Tunisia resort to the declaration of a state of emergency, not even at the height of the crisis. Nor did Tunisia promulgate ad hoc legislation to make terrorism the jurisdiction of just a few tribunals, to abridge procedures, or to reduce safeguards. Instead, Tunisia showed unbounded confidence in its courts and judges, treating those dangerous criminals simply as ordinary ones, allowing them all guarantees to defend themselves.

The Reinforcement of Audit and Control Institutions

The redistribution of power is not confined to a redistribution of the roles of the three traditional constitutional branches of government, but requires also the rehabilitation of the institutions of audit and control.

The first of these institutions is the Constitutional Council, which was set up on December 16, 1987, just a few months after the Change, and saw a gradual solidification of its legal status and terms of reference. On April 18, 1990, it ceased to be an internal institution of the executive branch and became a state institution, created by a legislative act that can only be abrogated or constrained by a new act.

Moreover, it has become compulsory for it to examine basic bills as well as legislation relating to general methods for the application of the Constitution, and to rights and liberties. Its findings are appended to the proposals, which are then submitted to the Chamber of Deputies. In this way, the government is obliged each time to amend proposed legislation to abide by the opinion of the Constitutional Council by eliminating any inconsistencies between the former and the latter.[96]

The Constitutional Council is made up of 9 members, who are competent jurisprudence men of integrity and impartiality, appointed by the President to include the First President of the Court of Cassation, the First President of the Administrative Court, and the President of the Court of Accounts, Tunisia's Auditor General. The current President of the Constitutional Council is the ex-First President of the Court of Cassation, reflecting a concern for safeguarding the independence of this institution and its legal mandate.

On November 7, 1994, the Seventh Anniversary of the Change, the President of the Republic stated his determination to modify the Constitution to provide for the Council. In July 1995, a draft law was submitted adding a new Article to the Constitution to provide for the Constitutional Council and reinforce its mandate. The Council was now a constitutional institution whose examination is required of basic bills, and of sensitive bills falling within the terms of reference of the Chamber of Deputies as guaranteed by Articles 34 and 35. The Council also reviews proposals for agreements. An explanation of these areas will reveal the Council's important role in protecting individual rights and securing a balance between all branches of government. The Council examines draft legislation relating to general methods for the application of the Constitution and to nationality, personal statute, covenants, the definition of crimes and sanctions, court procedures, legislative pardon, and the general principles of the ownership system, of personal rights, of education, of public health, of employment, and of social security. The Council also reviews draft legislation as defined in Article 47 of the Constitution and draft conventions as defined in Article 2 of the Constitution on referendums. Tunisia has made this choice to subject laws to a pre- rather than post-enactment review. The Council's review is compulsory in all these areas.

Unlike other comparable systems which have adopted the pre-enactment review, the system here does not make the jurisdiction of the Council dependent on cases referred to it by political authorities or by the representatives of the majority or minority.

Other projects are optionally submitted for review by the Council. However, for all reviews, the Constitutional Council's findings are brought before the Chamber of Deputies with the bills for the perusal of all deputies and the press. Therefore, the government is politically forced to bring its proposals in line with the views of the Constitutional Council and remove any incompatibilities with the Constitutions. That is because any contradictions will be exploited by the opposition in the Chamber of Deputies and by other political forces and journalists anxious to find grounds for criticism. Additionally, such contradictions could subsequently occasion a judicial rebuttal on the grounds of non-constitutionality. That is why the government is anxious to amend its proposals prior to bringing them before the Chamber of Deputies.

Between the April 28, 1990 Act defining the Constitutional Council's legislative competence and the end of 1990, 106 bills were submitted before the Council, 44 of which were returned to the government for incompatibilities with the Constitution to be ironed out. The Council's review role has become more and more forceful, returning one bill out of 11 for amendment in 1990, but 14 out of 23 bills brought before the Council in 1994.

All that is perhaps the most cogent illustration of Tunisia's pedagogically progressive approach to democracy: sagacious, prudent, gradual. No compulsion. No pressure. No fits and starts.[97]

Other institutions of audit and control are fired by a new dynamism. The Administrative Court, for instance, has become bolder and bolder in its decisions, revoking administrative provisions which had enjoyed limitless protection in the previous era.[98] There is an urgent need to subject the proceedings and decisions of the Administrative Court to a dual hierarchical structure and to establish its regional branches within citizens' reach throughout the Republic. As Ben Ali has announced, a project to do just that is underway.

The Court of Accounts and the Court of Fiscal Sanctions are busy catching up on belated issues of their reports in a bid to give their findings more effectiveness and their indictments more credibility. The President of the Court of Accounts as well as the President of the Supreme Institution of General Audits and Controls are often invited by the President to state their findings in general meetings attended by members of the cabinet and top-ranking government aides.

In addition, a portfolio of Commissioner for Administration, or Ombudsman, has been created. On December 18, 1992, a law creating the Department of the Ombudsman was enacted, reporting directly to the Presidency of the Republic alone. The Department of the Ombudsman has looked as mediator into individual administrative complaints from individuals and legal entities. In two years, they have received visits by 32,000 citizens creating 8,000 files, which have been refined into 6,800. The Administration acquiesced to the suggestions of the Commissioner for Administration in 56% of the cases, while in the other 44% its position proved to be justified. The above figures point to the level of confidence in, and credibility of, the institution as well as the regime.[99]

The picture on the audit and control system the state wants to install could not be complete without a discussion of the close attention to administrative work. The administration should be at the service of citizens, away from nepotism or favoritism. The Department of the Secretary of State for Administrative Reforms is in charge of Public Relations, of opening up PR offices in all the Ministries and important institutions, and of setting rules of conduct and efficiency standards for administrative services.

On January 26, 1993, Civilian-Operated Inspection Units were created within the Department of the Prime Minister to submit reports on shortcomings and merits of administrative service schedules, which are referred to the administration official in charge for appropriate action.

Ben Ali quickly realized the importance of the administration as a facet for the regime, that its public image has a determining influence upon popular attitudes to the regime as a whole. That is why he decided that administrative reform was not simply a technical, but primarily a political task, whose success was the most urgent requisite.

Hence, he has been busy making a series of unannounced visits to institutions, governmental and private, and to poor residential districts and rural areas. The visits have sparked live TV coverage that continually exposes the bureaucracy of the administration and excessive red tape and highlights at the same time the President's anxiety when the administration lags behind the progress he has made at the top of the state pyramid.

A New Role for the Ruling Party

At this stage of the Change, the redistribution of power is inextricably bound up with the reorganization of the ruling party. A salvation of the body politic could not be worked out, in the transition from unilateralism to pluralism, without saving the one party. There is a commonality of purpose and a parallelism of tasks, tempered in long years of cohesive and interdependent development.

Consequently, the tasks of the reform can only be carried out if the changes are to affect the machinery of the state as much as they are to affect the machinery of the ruling party. On July 31, 1988, during the Party Conference of Salvation, Ben Ali stated that he wanted "that Conference to be a truly decisive one." He said, "We have broken irretrievably with the errors of the past, and we have broken irrevocably with the mentality of the one party. Our party, for all its massive heritage, its established history of resistance, its wide electoral base, cannot claim to represent all the political forces of the country."

Because of that, and because he wanted everyone ready for the coming stage of political competition, Ben Ali was prudent to rebuild the single party and the state together, while other countries failed to prepare the single party for a pluralist climate, as they focused on the surface structures of the state and overlooked the party infrastructures underlying them.

Gorbachev's Soviet Union and Benjedid's Algeria are two cases in point.[100] Hence was born, in those cases, the confusion within the body politic and the resulting lack of the strong party support needed to provide the state with stability and generate popular mobilization down the new road. For in the one-party system, the state is a hollow edifice which, if unable to ground itself in a strong party that props it up, soon falls helplessly adrift in the incipient currents of the new forces and parties of extremism emerging in the wake of the previous regime.[101]

Tunisians would all agree Ben Ali saved the state as much as he saved the party, as he freed it from the grip of lethargy and state dependence. To its political discourse he brought renewal; to its leadership, change; to its veterans a revived spirit of criticism, and to its structures a new mood of initiative, enhancing its effectiveness and ability to compete with other parties, which had been expected to throw all their weight into the political battle to take advantage of the new climate prevailing in the wake of the November 7th Change.

In the early weeks of the Change, concurrently with the reforms of the state structure which had gotten underway, the ruling party was invigorated by intense, ongoing dynamism. The regime called upon a team of young political leaders, within the Political Bureau of the Party, to launch the rebuilding process by recruiting new blood, without giving up on existing, genuine expertise. Think-tank committees were set up with a mission to develop the party ideology, revitalize political discourse, and adapt working methods to the requirements of competitive, pluralist politics. Numerous national resources with varied specializations involved in the committees came to enrich the debate and energize the party with vigorous dynamism and spirited renewal. The movement culminated, in July, 1988, in what was called "the Salvation Conference," the first party conference in the new era of the Change.

A new start for the party of renewal, the kiss of life for a single body unopposed for 30 years, dwarfed by dark periods of servility and dependence, was on. A new name, the Democratic Constitutional Rally, instead of the old one, the Destourian

Socialist Party, came to mark at once continuity, by retaining the first term of the appellation, and renewal with the second term, signaling the democratic direction. The last term highlights the party's unionist character, seeking to stand for an open forum that rallies around all national forces dedicated to the Change. A new party leadership, a new political discourse, and new approaches to mobilization and methods of approach severed all links with the old ways of the past era.

There were those who had wanted, in the early days of the Change, to give up completely on the party and start a brand new one with no ties to the Destourian Socialist Party. Nevertheless, Ben Ali rejected that course of action, favoring a reform of the existing party that rebuilds it to conform with the new, pluralist direction. His famous words of that July 25 reverberate into the present: "The Democratic Constitutional Rally, the inheritor of the Constitutional Socialist Party, which has accrued the heritage of our people's history of resistance over 70 years, bears the special burden of making the experiment of democracy and pluralism a success. Here, as in other areas, we have opted for the principle of change in continuity, in the belief that no progress comes without the accumulative effect of experience.

"We have regenerated its structures, we have revitalized its programs and working methods, we have modernized its discourse by delving into the firmly established tradition of the liberation movement, we have reconciled its various generations, and reconciled it with society to empower it to discharge the responsibilities of this critical stage of our history. Therefore, with candor and clarity, we can say the Rally is the party of the President and the Party of the Change." That "the Rally is the party of the President and the Party of the Change" was a statement that took by surprise those who looked for a new party as well as November 7 Clubs.

Parallel events later showed that countries which embarked upon pluralism without a strong party met with great difficulties, with political ranks in disarray, lack of stability, and absence of the human element dedicated to mobilization and leadership. Liberalism thus gave way to hostile forces, every single voice heard save that which wanted the transformation, every single vision of the new society prominent save that behind the transformation.

True, the opposition leveled many criticisms at the Democratic Constitutional Rally, as the party, in their eyes, of continued, greater political hegemony and stronger mobilization. Nevertheless, the opposition itself gave up that line of criticism, realizing finally that the transition to pluralism cannot run true and innocent of distortion without a robust party that guarantees stability, that mobilizes the necessary political support to instill the principles of the change and stands vigilant against deviations and slips.

The events of 1992 in Algeria, and the successive events of 1991 in the Soviet Union, as well as other events, bespeak a concrete comparative lesson. The success of the Tunisian experience in the transition to pluralism vindicates the necessity of the strong regenerative party as the key factor to that transition.

One of the benefits the Democratic Constitutional Rally has reaped from the Change is a guarantee of its own survival, its now renewed discourse and working methodology making it well-equipped for the post one-party era. Today, in top form for the competition, it stands as a force to be reckoned with on major political occasions, significantly boasting a following of almost a quarter of the country's university lecturers, whereas it could only muster 1% of them in the early days of the Change. Similarly, student membership of the party has risen from a few hundred in 1987 to better than 8,000 in 1995. In 1993, total party membership stood at 1,720,374.

The party boasts 6,713 branches and 300 associations distributed across the Republic. There are 54,870 officials at branch level, 83,390 candidates having stood in the elections for local cell officials in 1993, i.e., 1.8 candidates per seat. Of that number, 4,400 were women, of whom 2,930 were elected—that is, 67% of the female candidates carried the day over their male counterparts. The election rate for a new local board reached 49%. Their educational qualifications were 40% primary education, 49% secondary education, and 11% university education. Seventy percent of them were aged 30 to 50. These indicators point to the dynamism and renewal of the party.[102]

The Democratic Constitutional Rally has been fortified not only by the new recruits among the national èlites and the young, two sectors that had a puny presence in the ruling party in the days of the old regime, but also by an increasingly wider popular base of sympathizers. That is because Tunisians today are not convinced of the need to belong to, or vote for, another party as they have found in the Rally the best guarantee for the implementation of Ben Ali's project. Such a state of affairs, to the credit of the ruling party, points to its regeneration and positive interaction with the Change, though its implications remain embarrassing for the opposition.

Tunisia's success in burnishing the party's potential, making of it a representative of the people's aspirations, embracing their worries throughout the land, which itself was the advocate of change, all made the party the best choice—and in danger of obviating the need for opposition movements. That is indeed one of the elements that later impeded the progress of democratic opposition, increasing the difficulties of recruitment and mobilization. Ben Ali recognizes that dilemma, and with the Democratic Constitutional Rally now sweeping across vast expanses of the political map, Ben Ali, who sees himself as the representative of all Tunisians, takes it upon himself to open up new opportunities before the opposition to enable it to coexist and excel, to ensure at least the equilibrium needed for fair political competition and a consolidated national dialogue between the party of the majority and the parties of the opposition in a climate that fosters all enriching contributions in the drive for modernization, affording citizens the best options available.[103]

The New Attitude to Non-Governmental Work

The road to pluralism also passes through the empowerment of non-governmental work, and through changing attitudes toward it. That work is neither a competitor nor an opponent of the regime, but an assistant and a supporter of it. Democracy demands of the state the release of initiative in the communal space to foster associations and clubs, social and intellectual dynamism, and a participation of a wide social base through which citizens can exercise their rights in the building of the nation.

New political discourse has been cultivated by mottos seeking to bolster civil society. Everyone is convinced that governmental work alone will not suffice, but should be supplemented by social work in all its forms. Nor can the political arena by itself achieve the new society. Governmental work must be solidified by cultural and social action. Acceptance of competition comes with training in cultural and social work, in youth clubs, in culture centers, and through voluntary work. As Ben Ali says, the rejection of extremism and fanaticism is a communal daily struggle, which requires not just the efforts of the government and its official apparatus, but also the participation of all the institutions of civil society and the exploitation of all communal forums and opportunities.

That is why the attitude of the government toward the creation of associations has changed, along with governmental relations to them. Basically, its attitude is no longer one of rejection, but one of encouragement and a desire to foster creation of the greatest possible number of civil forums in the various intellectual, scientific, sporting, social, and other arenas. Hence the rise we have seen earlier in the number of associations, which surpassed 5,200, concomitant with intensified association activities that make of them a teeming tributary to the Change. Many Non-Governmental Organizations (NGOs) have made Tunisia their headquarters, with many others choosing Tunisia as a site for their regional offices.[104]

On July 26, 1993, a new law was promulgated to expedite the setting up of NGOs in Tunisia and identify assistance services and privileges afforded them.

Non-governmental work is yet another jewel in the crown of Tunisia's triumph over extremism and fanaticism, favoring the emergence of a national pact and common political culture. Tunisia has managed to involve NGOs in the fight against fundamentalist ideology and its partisans. Some organizations infiltrated by extremist movements have been purged. And thus was born a new culture in the institutions of civil society, calling for a multi-cultural interaction, patriotism, and the respect of the other. With the contribution of NGOs, the defense is now an integrated, ongoing process involving culture centers, science clubs, voluntary organizations, and charity and humanitarian institutions as the stages of running battles against fanaticism.

Just for the record, then, Tunisian society has shown unparalleled awareness, quickly waking to the threat of fundamentalism once it was exposed. Every single outlet was mobilized first for the counter-offensive, and second for the inculcation of the new values brought by the November 7th Declaration, later refined into the National Pact, which was formulated with contributions from all political parties and major intellectual organizations and persuasions, and was co-signed by one and all, on November 7, 1988, just one year into the Change.[105]

The different forums of civil society had an essential part in rousing Tunisians' sensitivity against fanatic movements. Here, all parties have done the country a service that cannot but go down in history. There are those which from the beginning remained cautious and alert, staunch opponents rejecting the ideology of fanatic movements lock, stock, and barrel, and there are those who just flirted with it, while entertaining the hope of winning it over and taking its seats if it were to be deprived of participation in the elections.

Only later did they realize that fundamentalism was playing along with them, as a part of its tactics to avoid any political isolation in the eyes of public opinion at home and abroad. Then came the surprise to the leaders of those parties when they discovered blatant fundamentalist hypocrisy in their clandestine plotting to seize power by force. Mohamed Mouada, leader of one of those parties, then turned into a formidable adversary of fundamentalism. However, that uncertainty was not there for long as, by the end of 1991, the writing was on the wall: all national forces, including outlawed movements such as the Communist Party of Tunisian Workers, now came to a consensus on the need for a concerted stand against that movement, on the grounds that it represents a danger to democracy, to the Republican regime, and to the societal model to which all Tunisians aspire.

It is since that point that all closed ranks in the face of hostile foreign criticism and the stance taken by some human rights organizations. The Tunisian League for the Defense of Human Rights stood as an honorable example in this respect.[106]

In the light of its knowledge of the real designs of fundamentalist movements, the League refused to go along with comments propagated by certain foreign quarters and NGOs, initially, to the effect that they were movements of conscience and that their presence was no threat to the democratic process. Progressive forces within the League worked hard to purge its ranks of the dangerous element, rallying to rid the league of any stranglehold or distortion by fanaticism.

Other organizations, such as the Tunisian National Trade Union, and the Scout Association, as well as many others, in turn undertook similar purges of varying magnitude.

Another Role for the Elites

National elites had a major role to play in the Change, expressing allegiance to the principles and values of the November 7th Declaration. They readily enlisted in the battle to instill them and gave their backing to the regime to preserve the integrity and achieve the goals of that Declaration.

Those same elites had been averse to political action, remaining passive onlookers or negative critics. Some joined pan-Arab or left-wing opposition movements. Others joined humanitarian organizations as an alternative outlet for their political dissent. The majority, however, shunned political roles and civic activities. Tunisia is cited as a leading nation in the region, boasting a high rate of national educational and professional qualifications, an educated population with a schooling rate of 87%, and emancipated women, with an almost equal number of male and female students at university.

That unquenched thirst for political action and that feeling of exclusion from, or guilt at inadequate participation in, the national effort, was perhaps what made the elites, immediately after the Change, rush to intellectual forums, seek all and any opportunities or outlets to work within governmental institutions, the ruling party structures, or the opposition lines.

Attitudes also changed toward the participation of the elites in the activities of the regime. That participation had earlier been regarded as a form of worship of power, and flattery designed to butter up the powers that be for coveted positions. And truth to tell, that sort of conduct did appeal to a number of people, some of whom came to lose credibility in their fields of specialization. Such a view, though not true in all cases, did harm to the regime by depriving it of distinguished expertise. By contrast, attitudes were completely reversed after the Change. The elites now took pride in helping the project for the new society come to fruition. The national higher cadre, without exception whatsoever, derive a special pleasure from that involvement, because the doors are now open for real change, all sectors are in need of development, and the data bank for proposals is far from being saturated. In fact, competition is now on among the highly qualified elites to give the best of themselves. One need only review ministerial portfolios or top-ranking government posts or important institutional management to see the remarkable contingent of high caliber personnel there.

Detailed figures are more apt to reveal the extent of Ben Ali's near total reliance on competence. That ability to recruit national qualified resources whether at home or working abroad, explains to some extent Tunisia's unprecedented success in rates of development and in addressing political issues, including that of paving the way to pluralism. If you happened to enter Ben Ali's private office, you will find yourself in the presence of a vast array of computers and computer diskettes, including the National Data Bank of Qualified Expertise, which is compiled on the basis of various searches and questionnaire surveys.

Qualified specialists and scientists abroad have also received personal attention from Ben Ali, who invites a number of them over on important national occasions, calling upon them to preserve ties with the homeland so as best to serve it.

The expertise of specialists was not beneficial merely through direct appointments to top-ranking positions, but more importantly, the involvement of such expertise in important fora of debate was an asset in preparing the ground for national policies. That is because Ben Ali pays great heed to the advice of experts, follows up fastidiously on reports submitted to him, and is as intent on being informed of assenting views as he is of dissenting ones.[107]

A political system's ability to harness national expertise is a telling barometer, as the more proficient it is at recruiting that expertise, the more efficient it is in accomplishing its objectives and rising to the challenges ahead at a minimum cost. That is an aspect which has been rather ignored by analysts, while, in our view, it is a prerequisite for the evaluation of any regime's viability, and particularly those regimes intent, as Tunisia is, to catch up with advanced societies, to achieve rapid and comprehensive progress within a free democratic society.[108]

A regime's efficiency is fortified if power is ideally distributed. Centralization and the personality cult kill the regime. The more the distribution of roles between the different branches is transparent and the opportunities for participation are thrown wide open, the more resources are fired up and enthusiasm mustered in the service of the public good and for the defense of the nation's achievements.[109]

Nevertheless, the internal balance still requires a sturdier opposition, capable of standing as a viable alternative, and of rallying people around it. And that remains President Ben Ali's nagging preoccupation.

The New Political Culture

The redistribution of power is a measure that acts not only upon institutions and policies, but must also influence the prevalent political culture inside the party in power, and, equally, inside opposition circles.[110] Hence, the process of institutional reforms must be accompanied by a new political culture.

Yet the inculcation of the new political culture is not as simple as one might believe; it is the most intricate and far-reaching of the reforms, over a long time-frame that spans one if not more generations. For that process involves changing values and traditions: those of the leadership in power, those of the opposition leadership, as well as those of the people involved by them in the broader realms of society.

Ben Ali has found himself often pondering ways and means for the transition from the culture of the one-party system to that of pluralism. He knows only too well that three decades of one- party hegemony have left their imprint on political life in Tunisia, and that removing their residues will require a long time and unrelenting effort.[111]

One should not jump to the conclusion that the one-party mentality is one that affects the leadership and partisans of the one-party rule alone, since it usually marks also the patterns of behavior of those dealing with them as well as those in the opposition parties and in fora of civil society. All those patterns need to be modified.[112]

The ruling party, by virtue of governing uncontested, will have acquired a deep-seated disposition to rely on, and passively await action by, the state, not showing any qualms over abusing the law if the opportunities arose. The opposition is consequently invested with a similar disposition, learning in time to rely on, and passively await action by, the state on the off-chance that it might do something to lift its siege and allow the opposition to catch up. The opposition also explains any failure that befalls it by the domination of the ruling party. It does not seek to build its own policies, to formulate an agenda outlining its objectives, but just criticizes the policies of the majority party. It thus fails to put forward alternatives to, or to compete with, the ruling party. Instead, it merely clings to the policies of the ruling party, content with criticizing it and complaining of its conduct.

The man in the street, who deals with one and the other, and makes comparisons between them, is hard put to find alternative policies or a clear debate that explains his options. He has no choice but to not take the opposition seriously, or find it too fragile to offer innovation, not strong enough at any rate to inspire his enthusiasm and win his sympathy. The ruling party remains in his eyes dominant in the political arena, but at the same time an effective regenerative force without which the formulation or implementation of serious policies is just unthinkable.

Therefore, there was not a sufficient degree of the culture of competition established on the basis of initiative, self-reliance, and the search for excellence in the design of programs and slogans. In the wake of the last municipal elections of May 21, 1995, when the opposition failed to obtain a significant number of seats, an objective line of criticism, first articulated by the Renewal Movement in a statement addressed to the President on June 5, 1995, pointed to just that crisis in political culture. The statement argued the opposition needed to liberate itself of negative criticism, to lay the foundations of an alternative positive approach with a capacity to appeal and mobilize. It also criticized the attitude of dominance which still marked some of the local structures of the ruling party that did not align themselves with the pluralist directions Ben Ali had in mind. It suggested that such a state of affairs did not serve pluralism, that a rapprochement of views and attitudes had to be worked, in order that we might achieve the pluralist society the November 7th Declaration seeks to establish.

Moreover, the new regime would like to see new values, new mores of competition, and new standards of dialogue prevail over political interaction between parties as foundations for a new political culture to befit the desired pluralist society. Ben Ali had already summed those up on the first Anniversary of the Change in a speech addressed to the Symposium on Democratic Changes in the World Today. He referred to that culture as the culture of consensus, and called the desired democracy the democracy of consensus. That democracy is not the classic one, where the logic of numbers means the majority rules and the minority complies, but a new kind of democracy where the right of the majority to govern is respected, without a marginalization of the minority, whose views are taken on board wherever possible. That is exactly what Ben Ali has been doing on major issues. Of course, he does base himself on the majority rule, within his party, the Democratic Constitutional Rally. Nevertheless, as frequently as possible, he listens to the opinions of the other parties, seeks their advice on basic policies, invites them to take part in major debates, and entrusts them with various duties and specific national missions.

Now we get to the crucial stage on the road to pluralism, the tough challenge of rehabilitating democratic opposition to strengthen its competitive powers, that it might contribute to the political balance and offer individuals and society greater opportunities for a varied choice. □

THE THIRD CHALLENGE:
The Rehabilitation of Democratic Opposition

THIS IS THE ULTIMATE link in Ben Ali's strategic trinity. Having repelled the movements pulling the Change toward a new unilateralism, having redistributed power to prepare the ground for the pluralist stage, it now remains to initiate another key process on the road to pluralism, and that is the rehabilitation of democratic opposition to fill the political gap left behind by the previous one-party regime.

We use the word rehabilitation in the meaning of the French term *"réhabilitation,"* i.e., creating the conditions for a healthy opposition to evolve and acquire greater and greater capacity forcefully to enter the competition and take full advantage of the political liberalization being gradually offered by the new era.

Political Liberalization and the Risk of Swallowing up the Opposition

Observers generally still labor under the misapprehension that political liberalization after periods of repression opens up opportunities for democratic opposition and offers it a better platform for competition and a greater ability to win over points and seats. This notion is indeed misguided, since in nascent democracies it is extremist movements which tend to benefit the most from the sudden liberalization. They are usually more adept at assimilating popular anger and railroading the change onto whichever route they choose. They will have a secret branch ready and waiting to come into the open to reinforce their public wing. The various oppressed classes, saturated in years of accumulated anger, are at this point more apt than ever to be swept away by extremism, ever driven to excess, ready to stand behind movements which promise swift and radical changes and bandy about catchy slogans to satisfy all desires and fulfill all aspirations. They are eager for radical, sweeping reforms and are carried away by those movements which vow to be even more extremist, even more revolutionary in overturning the old ways.

At the same time, balanced democratic opposition has not acquired a recognizable shape to be able to steer and channel popular demands, to work out more plausible alternatives to the existing choices. Now, democratic movements are not yet ready. Reason not being the order of the day, it is an uphill struggle to rationalize ambitions, to get people to listen to figures, or to influence their political attitudes. To make matters worse, just after the Change, democratic opposition parties were in disarray. Some were outlawed and needed the ban on them to be lifted, others were recognized but still delicate and fragile, requiring assistance in the refinement of their programs and in their efforts to reorganize, to form a more solid base, and to win over a greater number of sympathizers.

At the time of the Change, Ben Ali was faced with anti-democratic movements that did not believe in the republican values, and looked to pounce on power and divert the change to serve its interests. The most important of those was the Movement of the Islamic Tendency. The key dictum of that movement was that Islam, as it saw it, was the way to salvation, that the application of its distorted vision of the divine *Shari'a* law was the best guarantee of a safe society and a prosperous economy. As discussed earlier, it is set on establishing a totalitarian regime that regiments man's life down to the minutest detail, including styles for dressing, haircuts, and beard length. In the eyes of this movement, and of fundamentalism in general, democracy is heresy, because it means the government of man, whereas government is the preserve of God alone. However tactful fundamentalist leaderships are in their public rhetoric toward other opinions, however outwardly accepting of democracy, that cannot be but tactical, transitory assertions. For religious systems, deep inside, are animated by a narrow, totalitarian philosophy that believes in nothing but what in their views constitute divine pronouncements.

Because of the previous regime's isolation and neglect of Islam, the fundamentalist movement was able to manipulate deep-rooted popular religious feeling, to pander to various sectors of the population possessed by misery and despair.

For that reason, any improvised political liberalization will in the first stages of the change provide such a movement with the democratic space it needs to impose itself upon the political scene by winning over to its cause the angry and the discontented. In the name of democracy, that movement is in the long run able to kill democracy, and to return to a new kind of monolithic system, more entrenched and more dangerous.

What makes the *Nahdha* Movement even more dangerous is its reliance, like all fundamentalist movements that have sprouted up in the region, on foreign funding and its use of violence to have its way. It charges anyone who does not vote for it with heresy, throwing at the electorate the book of God to obtain their vote.

That is at least what happened during the legislative elections of 1989 in Tunisia, when fundamentalists stood for election on independent lists. We have dwelled extensively on this aspect in the first part of this book.

Beside the *Nahdha*, another outlawed movement is the Communist Party of Tunisian Workers, a clandestine, extremist organization, which also does not believe in republican values, and aims to found a classless society where state authority just dissolves. Neither does that party believe in democracy or majority rule. Instead, it believes in the dominance of the working classes. For these reasons, which violate the law on political parties, that party did not manage to obtain the necessary legal permit to operate.

The Communist Party of Tunisian Workers is a Marxist-Leninist organization with a Stalinist bent, and similarities with the Albanian Workers' Party which formerly ruled Albania.

It was set up in the early '80s (1982), as an extension to the extreme left-wing organizations in Tunisia, particularly the organization of "The Tunisian Worker," which was itself an off-shoot of Perspectives, a movement that was founded in the middle of the 1960s. The Communist Party believes in the dictatorship of the proletariat, and "the struggle for basic liberties" is just one of many stages on its strategic activist agenda.

Approximate figures, since the movement operates in secrecy, reveal the Communist Party of Tunisian Workers to have a following of 5,000 members. Its organizational structure is a closed top-down hierarchy, where activists are not known to each other, and grouped into separate, discrete cells.[113] The party does not constitute a major movement on the Tunisian political scene, and is unknown to most people.

The Communist Party took part in the legislative elections of 1989 on independent lists, and in the same manner in the municipal elections of 1990, where it chronicled a relative revival in Denden, Mornaguia, Monastir, Hamma, and Hammam Sousse. Thanks to funding and resources obtained in Zeramdine and Shebba, it was able to take the majority of seats in the municipality of Chebba. The party finds recruits among partisans of the left. Recognizing it would amount to reducing the chances of the moderate left, which all democracies need.

In a statement issued on May 1, 1991, the Communist Party declared the need to wage a continued war on the regime that razes it to the ground. Through its offshoot, the Organization of Communist Youth, it called for its partisans to rouse revolutionary awareness. Then, looking to explore relations with the *Nahdha* Movement, the Communist Party of Tunisian Workers decided to engage in talks with it without descending below a certain level of sobriety, as the *Nahdha* had embarked upon a direct and bloody confrontation with the regime. The coalition, however, led to a division inside the Party, which became apparent in two well-known statements, referred to as Number 41.

Tunisia has always been of the opinion that pluralism does not come by opening the floodgates to such extremist movements. There must be a period of transition when the course of the Change has to be subject to control, so as not to allow those movements, which, because of their extremism, are more able to mobilize discontent with captivating but hollow slogans. At this point, such movements have a capacity to swell, drawing around them marginalized groups and attracting votes. Such votes are not votes of conviction, but votes cast in anger at the old regime.

One researcher went so far as to say that in the aftermath of the fall of totalitarian regimes voting is totalitarian too, either accepting the system in totality or rejecting the system wholesale, without discrimination among the programs or alternatives offered. They are votes that seek not to give total support to extremist movements, but to find an actual outlet for their wrath against the old system of government.

That is why Tunisia has opted to control the channels of democracy, deciding not to turn on the tap all the way, so to speak, but just enough to allow the healthy, democratic opposition to benefit. The risk has never been at any time to the ruling party, the Democratic Constitutional Rally, since Ben Ali had seen to it that his party was rebuilt with a sharpened competitive drive and a secure majority rooting for it. The real risk has always been to democratic opposition, which might not be in a position during this transition period to find a sizable, sensible, rational base capable of enough discrimination and far-sightedness to resist being carried away by the slogans and fantastic promises offered to voters by the advocates of extremism.

At the end of the day, in the absence of democratic opposition and the emergence of uncontested extremist opposition, the attitudes of each side are increasingly hardened, causing a precarious rift in the political texture of the country, since there now is no common ground between that opposition and the ruling party for competition and dialogue to take place. Instead, there emerge on the political map two drastically opposed poles that tear asunder nationals of the same, one country, driving them into more and more entrenched positions. Rather than a steady progress toward pluralism and fair exchanges, there is a rapid return to a one-party system in an even more rigid and aggressive form, which may well result in conflict and civil strife. Francis Fukuyama, who sees "the end of history" in the triumph of liberal democracy over all other systems, dwells particularly on fundamentalism, which he feels is "the gravest threat to liberal practice, even in those countries where it has not seized power."[114]

He adds (page 387) that "in this part of the world [the Middle East], Islamic fundamentalism has become the greatest stumbling block to democracy." He then goes on to say that the events in Algeria and earlier in Iran have shown that greater democracy does not lead to greater liberalism, because it leaves the way open to the rule of Islamic fundamentalism, which is still hoping to pull off a victory that establishes a popular theocracy (or so he called it), "diametrically opposed to liberal democracy" (page 388).

It is in the light of that background that the observer has to assess Tunisia's gradual progression along the way to political liberalization. He has to measure what the democratic process has achieved by the yardstick of the risks attached to too hasty a liberalization. Ben Ali's strategy deserves a more thorough scrutiny for analysts to appreciate and evaluate the merits of the democratic transformation in one-party societies from a new perspective. For that strategy's clear vision accounts for its deliberate, gradual pace. By contrast, other societies have approached liberalization with such indecisive policies, such retreats on the part of leaders, such a hasty implementation, that they fell into deviations. Tunisia's strategy, on the other hand, has allowed her to avert the risks of a crisis, availed her of greater opportunities for freedom and prosperity, and enabled her to make giant strides on the road to pluralism. Undoubtedly, she has not gone all the way, but hers is a genuine progression toward pluralism, drawing ever nearer to a better performance.

To simplify Tunisia's approach to pluralism, one must imagine Ben Ali momentarily closing the door on a charging anti-democratic current, allowing it to remain open just enough to allow democratic opposition to come in and catch its breath after strenuous efforts. As for the Democratic Constitutional Rally, having set its own house in order and restored it to full capacity, he can rest assured of its integrity, away from any conflict. The democratic opposition today knows full well that the political equation centers around an overt protagonist, that is the Rally, and a covert player, that is the extremist movements. It knows too that the gradual progression in opening up competition is not meant to protect the ruling party, but to protect the democratic opposition, lest extremist movements swallow up their chances of survival.

One need only review the succession of decisions taken to feel Ben Ali's special interest in rehabilitating the democratic alternative, preparing the ground for competition, and filling the gap left behind by the previous regime. That gap must be filled by those who are democratic, not those who are anti-democratic. Since the anti-democratic legions are ready and the democratic one just getting ready, it follows that gradual progression is essential to sort out those who can benefit from the democratic liberalization.

Immediately after the Change, the regime set about opening the way to democratic opposition. On September 12, 1988, the Progressive Socialist Rally and the Social Party for Progress obtained their permits, followed by the Unionist Democratic Union, on November 30, 1988. The regime also broke the stranglehold that was suffocating three older parties: the Renewal Movement; the former Communist Party of Tunisian Workers, which was recognized on July 19, 1981, but remained subject to restricted movement and did not participate in major political events; and the Socialist Democratic Movement and the Popular Unity Party, which obtained their permits on November 19, 1983, but proved ineffective in obtaining a sufficient base of supporters.

The opposition parties and the ruling party are now brought together in partnership, not in enmity. Ben Ali sees them as an integral part of the regime, an essential player to the democratic contest, and an official institution. That is why he calls upon his party to deal with them as a political partner. One significant and symbolic aspect of that new relationship, for example, is the invitation of every opposition party's Secretary General to attend national ceremonies, and take part in major events. The President of the Republic receives them regularly for consultation on various issues in the context of the new pluralist direction we have discussed earlier.

Now, we must turn to the institution of the political structures of the democratic opposition. Some opposition parties have lost parts of their slogans and agendas, which had been taken over as part of the greater project initiated by Ben Ali. Others have lost a few of their leaders, who became convinced that remaining in the opposition made no sense, that a direct participation in the new regime served better the principles and values they had fought for. That was particularly true of the Socialist Democratic Movement and parties of an Arabist persuasion.

The mosaic of democratic political forces could not be complete without a description of the dynamism that marked Tunisia's restructuring efforts after the Change. The emergence of democracy after 30 years of the one-party system compelled the opposition to reposition itself, to modernize its discourse, to adopt a new working methodology, to canvass for new supporters, and to train its leaders to adapt to the new open, public climate of competition.

Major political events implicating the opposition parties, notably the elections, have shown the need for greater coordination among them and with the government, as well as the need for alliances. Hence, thinking has moved in the direction of bringing together certain intellectual families. The formation of a troika comprising three parties to take part in the municipal elections of May 21, 1995, was an experiment that showed the merits of coalition, but also the need to prepare that coalition sufficiently in advance. The three were the Popular Unity Party, the Renewal Movement, and the Unionist Democratic Rally.

An additional difficulty being experienced by the democratic opposition is the ideological vacuum left behind by the old one-party system. Tunisia had lived for 30 years without political thought being able to take form, to acquire distinctive features, or to follow clear lines that would have enabled opposition parties to vie with each other to mobilize public opinion. Those years of political tyranny had so weakened the opposition movements, both organizationally and ideologically, that none was able to survive, even under the surface, save for the clandestine extremist ideologies, such as the *Nahdha* Movement and the Communist Party of Tunisian Workers.

Therefore Ben Ali concluded that the opposition in Tunisia today has a vital role to play, which is to lay the foundations of political thought to compete with that of the ruling party, to rise to the challenge of drawing mass support around it, and to fill out the democratic ideological vacuum. That mission is not at all straightforward, since it requires of the opposition leadership and elite a much greater effort. Ideological competition between all political parties, in power and out, is the catalyst which generates a dynamic which commands the attention of all, motivates participation in election issues, and invites the comparison of distinctive programs and concrete alternatives.

That ideological vacuum reflects negatively upon the media. Newsmen need material, as much as viewers need convincing arguments. Parties bring an essential, enriching contribution to the dialogue, and add spice to questions provoking public opinion. In large part, criticism leveled today by observers toward the media is also directed at the elites of all parties, which have not provided the necessary material for an interesting and persuasive debate that really engages viewers.

We turn to the democratic opposition parties, which, it will be noted, each have their own organizational and ideological peculiarities. Analysts should not see them from an immutable perspective, but as rapidly evolving political parties with expanding recruitment capacities, greater financial resources, and growing leadership and elite expertise and experience. In 1994, the number of democratic opposition headquarters reached 250, 149 of which belonged to the Socialist Democratic Movement, 36 to the Popular Unity Party, 23 to the Renewal Movement, 22 to the Unionist Democratic Union, 14 to the Progressive Socialist Rally, 6 to the Social Party for Progress. The number of leading opposition figures was better than 1,800.

The Renewal Movement is believed to be the oldest opposition party. It came into being to replace the defunct Tunisian Communist Party, which was in turn an extension of the Tunisian branch of the French Communist Party founded in the early '20s. The party was revived in 1993 to accommodate the events that have affected Marxism, and more generally the left the world over, adopting the new name, the Renewal Movement. The Communist Party of Tunisian Workers had taken part in the elections of 1981 and 1986.[115] The Renewal Movement is a "patriotic democratic movement," which aspires to be "the first nucleus of a wider movement that shall be nothing but progressive, rational, and modern."[116]

During its conference of April, 1993, the Renewal Movement was successful in adjusting to the new situation of the world left. It pulled away from the extremist left and its rigid rhetoric and was able to go along with the competitive pluralist direction, which requires it to share the values of other parties, without losing its left-wing character in its perception of the free market economy, its relations with labor movements, and so on. The Renewal Movement has drawn toward the center to avoid alienation from the political arena and to be nearer the everyday life of the people. Nevertheless, the rigid left-wing elements who had experienced the leftist rhetoric of the '60s and '70s, from Stalin to Enver Hoxha, refused to be associated with the movement. The Renewal Movement has a newspaper called *"The New Road."* Still, it may be useful to explore the sociology of the left, affiliations and membership after the November 7th Change, and the reasons behind apathy to this movement. It is also notable that many well-known left-wing figures have preferred to join the Democratic Constitutional Rally at the service of Ben Ali's project.

The Popular Unity Party goes back to the '70s when "The Progressive Activists," as they prefer to be called, started a protest against the policies of liberal economy. In 1977, a number of them were brought to trial. In 1981, the party applied for a permit, which it obtained in November, 1983. It is a separate organization from the Popular Unity Party, which was associated with the Co-operative experiment in the '60s, as it came and went with it. The Popular Unity Party's distinctive position is its reservations about a free economy and emphasis on social equality. An internal party document, dated November 23, 1992 and submitted to the Organization of Progressive Socialist Parties, identified the Movement's objectives as follows:

- To institute democracy on a larger scale in everyday (Tunisian) life.

- To bolster economic interdependence between the peoples of the Mediterranean.
- To work to achieve self-sufficiency for our peoples, and gradually reduce unwarranted economic dependence.

The party has also spelled out details of its programs in the Charter, in the Ideological Guidelines, and in the Popular Liberties Charter (Sfax Conference, December 7, 1986). The party convenes its conference every three years, and has a Central Council comprising 50 members elected by the conference, which convenes every four months. The Council elects a Political Bureau of 7 members, which is in charge of running the party. It is also in charge of electing Secretaries General for the 17 associations, who join the Political Bureau, together with the Chairmen of the five committees, in a wider formation to look into major issues. The party has a newspaper called *"The Union,"* with 10,000 copies issued.

The Socialist Democratic Movement was established on June 10, 1978, by liberal activists, some of whom had broken away from the ruling party, the then Destourian Socialist Party. The Movement, which obtained legal recognition in December, 1983, had been demanding pluralist democracy. It took part in the elections of 1981, and was able to get a sizable proportion of the vote. The Movement campaigns for three objectives: democracy, socialism, and an Arab Islamic identity. It shares almost the same beliefs with the Democratic Constitutional Rally. However, on the economic front, it still harks back to socialist policies of control. An example of that is its attachment to the public sector, provided it is rationalized and made profitable. Another example is its use of slogans like the struggle against the exploitation of workers by employers, and independence from international capitalism.

The Socialist Democratic Movement also stands out for its pan-Arab tendencies. The Movement's Charter (March 28, 1993) commits it to the following:

- To strive to make democracy the basis of everyday life in the country and to wage a relentless battle against injustice, violence, and intolerance.
- To resist man's exploitation of man and fight to install a socialist regime that utilizes economic development in the service of social equity.
- To work to reinforce the Arab Islamic identity of the Tunisian people, and to strengthen their civilizational and future links to the Arab nation.
- To defend the republican system and the independence of the country.

The National Conference is the highest authority of the Movement. It convenes every five years, whereas a National Council follows up on the implementation of the resolutions of the Conference. The Council comprises 90 members, and convenes every six months. It elects a Political Bureau composed of 19 to 25 members. The Bureau follows up on the implementation of policies and decisions, and oversees the administration of the Movement. There is an Executive Secretariat which emanates from the Political Bureau, comprising 7 to 9 members, of whom one is the Chairman of the Movement, and carries out the day-to-day activities of the Movement in the various fields. Every three months, the Political Bureau assembles in a generalized formation comprising the Secretaries- General of the Movement's associations. The Movement publishes a regular newspaper called *"The Future."*

The Unionist Democratic Union is relatively young, since it was recognized on November 30, 1988. However, it represents a unionist tradition which is well-established. The Union enjoys close relations with pan-Arab movements, which should be seen in the context of "organizational and political independence," as the Secretary General of the Union argues. The Union aims to achieve a Confederation of the Arab World, based on democracy and mutual respect of each Arab country's particularities. The Union differs from most other unionist movements in the Arab world in that it bases union on democracy. It also believes economic interdependence to be a basis for political unity. The Union's Conference convenes every three years and elects a National Council, which assembles every four months. It also elects its Political Bureau, which comprises 11 members and is the top-level structure of the Union.

The Progressive Socialist Rally was founded on November 13, 1983, and could only obtain its permit after the Change, on September 12, 1988. It follows a pan-Arab unionist tendency, and has a progressive leftist character. It took part in the legislative elections of 1989 and 1994. It has a Central Committee composed of 30 members elected by the Conference, which convenes every three months and deliberates and decides on party policy.

The Committee elects the Political Bureau, which is composed of seven permanent members, and six other members regularly elected by the Central Committee. The Political Bureau decides on major political positions of the party and is in charge of following up on the activities of its structures.

No member of the Bureau is able to undertake a political mission without the express approval of the Central Committee. The Central Committee also elects the Secretary General of the Rally, which has a National Consultative Council that assembles once a year. The party publishes a paper called *"The Position."*[117]

The Liberal Social Party was recognized on September 12, 1988. It has a completely liberal ideology. However, its organizational capacities are still moderate. It took part in the legislative elections of 1989 and 1994, and in the municipal elections of 1995, on one list in the city of Ksar Gafsa. The party publishes a paper called *"The Horizon."*

The presence of the opposition is still modest. Its ideologies and programs still need refinement and marketing. Nevertheless, its presence has been sufficient to change the country's model of government as well as the patterns of political conduct. Its capacities are being steadily bolstered, the extremists who eat up its space and hunt on its territory having been firmly grounded.

Funding and the Risk of Erosion

However, opposition parties, truth to tell, still lack financial support. Their tiny, fragile membership cannot provide them the funding they need to finance their own canvassing campaigns and carry seats in electoral contests. On the other hand, their limited political presence prevents them from effecting greater human mobilization and consolidating their financial resources and assets. Hence, time is needed to bring them out of this vicious circle.

In a bid to accelerate the progress of the opposition, the government has come up with the idea of giving assistance to the opposition parties in order that they might fulfill their political function to the best of their ability and contribute to the building of a balanced society. That is because the opposition has a vital role to play in building democracy and therefore bringing stability and prosperity to society. In one-party systems, democratic opposition additionally fulfills a special role, as it is called upon to fill the political gap and close the door on extremism. Thus, the Electoral Code provides for the state to give the opposition parties a grant to help them participate in legislative and presidential electoral campaigns. Half of that grant is received before standing for election, and the other half after the elections, except for lists which obtain less than 3% of the votes of the electoral district, or less than 5% in presidential elections. In municipal elections, all ballot-printing expenses are reimbursed for all except lists with less than 3% of the vote. In practice, the state undertakes all printing and distribution to voting stations, free of charge. The government also subsidizes the opposition press, by bearing 60% of the paper cost of opposition party newspapers. In 1991, the President of the Republic took a decision to allocate to the opposition newspapers a grant to the tune of 30,000 dinars to enable them to meet publication costs. In addition, opposition party newspapers have the benefit of the facilities routinely granted to all newspapers, such as free train transportation, air-mail transportation at a 50% discount, reduced rates for hotel board, significant reductions in customs tariffs levied on equipment and other newspaper printing material, and a 50% discount on both wire and wireless local and international communications for institutions of the press.

Subsidies, however, cannot be that large, given the limited resources of the state. On the other hand, they cannot exceed the parties' assimilation capacities, nor can they negatively affect their independence. They are just suited to the parties' campaigning potential and political activities and enough to cover the parties' participation in major electoral events. Subsidies also carry the risk of getting used to reliance and dependence on the state. This last argument makes it best for parties to rely on themselves to raise independent resources, even if that requires time and sacrifice.

Therefore it has become urgent for opposition parties, of course as their leaderships see fit, to energize their political action and increase their membership to a degree that will bring in even greater support and attain financial independence and resources to fund their activities.

That has already started, so that the opposition should be able, within a few years, to break the vicious circle described earlier, assisted particularly by its presence in the Chamber of Deputies.

For Parliament has won the opposition greater popularity and enhanced credibility and afforded it a prominent platform to enlarge its activist ranks and increase its financial resources.

Therein lies the dilemma of the government. It has to help the opposition without eroding its credibility, to subsidize it without causing its parties to become dependent. For this reason, Ben Ali is anxious to create the appropriate climate for opposition to grow on its own steam, to bolster its activism while maintaining its independence and credibility. Now, thinking may move in the direction of passing a law to secure a minimum level of public funding for political parties, with contributions from the state budget to expenses incurred in election campaigns, which are indeed a heavy burden on the shoulders of candidates.

From Armchair Criticism to the Public Arena

One fact, certainly undeniable, is that the new regime took on board most of the opposition programs and maxims, which it incorporated into the wider, more explicit project formulated by Ben Ali and endorsed by the Democratic Constitutional Rally, in the Salvation Conference of July 31, 1988, its first conference.[118] That is because Ben Ali insists on taking the lead in the policy of change that he has adopted to meet the demands and ambitions of the people. Hence, he has reduced the scope for criticism before the opposition parties, and increased the ranks of party supporters and sympathizers.

On the other hand, the ruling party's revival, its renewed discourse and working methodology, have had an adverse effect on the size of the opposition. As the Rally increased its mobilized following, the opposition in general, and the democratic opposition in particular, lost ground and opportunities for action.

All these changes have meant that the democratic opposition has to develop the stamina needed to institutionalize a new tradition. More precisely, observers think, it has to adapt to the new variables. The opposition, as it realizes itself, cannot make material progress in just a few years. Its participation in the elections, as it rightly points out, aims to create a dynamism that is as self-serving as it is beneficial to the political community as a whole.

Despite the limited number of seats it usually obtains, its participation in electoral campaigns has provided it with training and a consolidated base of partisans, with greater opportunities to put forward its own political case, to fine-tune its discourse to the new reality, and to train its leaders and activists. That is what has boosted the potential of opposition parties, to evolve away from armchair criticism and out into the real world, on to opposition in the public arena, with a style that captures the interest and imagination of supporters.

The presence of the opposition in the Chamber of Deputies during the 1994 session undoubtedly prepares the ground, in our estimate, for a more imposing presence in 1999, since there is an interrelated, positive, dynamic cycle whereby parties gain strength in the field through their presence in decision-making institutions, and their presence in decision-making institutions is reinforced through their strength in the field. The setback suffered by the opposition in the municipal elections of 1995 can be traced back, in our view, to its preparations not being made sufficiently in advance, and to its eagerness to score a victory on a wide scale, which scattered its efforts and therefore weakened its chances of winning seats. In fact, it could have won several municipality seats, if only it had focused better and planned better, if it had taken its time to think through its electoral campaigns.

The opposition's eagerness for more seats is legitimate and desirable from a competitive standpoint. The majority party's endeavor to preserve its lead is also legitimate and desirable. The road to pluralism that Ben Ali has paved is the correct one. As pluralism has been irrevocably established, extremism has been irrevocably excluded. And when the vacuum is filled, when the democratic parties share most of the social and ideological map and the body of supporters and sympathizers, then, and only then, will extremism have run out of options, deprived of a murky corner in which to nestle, or of a putrescent soil upon which to feed.

From the Philosophy of Looking On to the Philosophy of Joining In

The opposition parties have found in their adopted philosophy of joining in, a pragmatic, fruitful philosophy to replace the philosophy of looking on and boycotts. This positive choice has enabled them, despite their relatively recent history, to impose themselves and steadily increase their following in the different districts and social strata.

There now appeared in the discourse of the ruling party, as much as in that of the opposition, new concepts referring to joint action and a culture of partnership. They are concepts whose aim is to bring national democratic forces at this juncture of the Change closer and closer, to banish anything and everything that will sow division or cause cracks in the edifice of the new society.

From the early months following the Change, Ben Ali hastened to codify the values and principles that must unite all Tunisians, to set down the standards of political conduct that best serve the first stage of pluralism.

He therefore called for the formulation of a National Pact to take place with contributions from all the intellectual and political persuasions. On November 7, 1988, the National Pact was co-signed by all the parties, trade unions, and representatives of the major humanitarian organizations and intellectual trends. The National Pact is a political contract, a written consensus which all protagonists have pledged to respect.

The National Pact has promoted a consensus of otherwise opposed views, by highlighting what unites Tunisians, and discarding what divides them. That consensus is essential for the installation and survival of democracy, as without an agreement on the major values and principles, on the standards of political conduct, competition will turn into conflict, democracy into a senseless discord that finally tears up the social fabric and dissipates stability.[119]

The National Pact has laid down values and principles which have come to occupy a prominent place in the literature of all parties. Here are some of them:

- The adoption of democracy, based on intellectual and organizational pluralism, as an irrevocable system of government.
- The recognition and respect of the right to difference and to a different opinion, and the protection of rights of minorities.
- The adoption of tolerance as a guiding principle of relations between Tunisians and the exclusion of all manifestations of fanaticism and violence.
- The commitment of all Tunisians to strive to go beyond anything that might disunite them in order to create a climate of national solidarity that fosters the reconciliation of all.
- Tunisia's commitment to its Arab identity and pledge to promote the Arabic language while maintaining openness to other languages and cultures; and Tunisia's commitment also to Islam as a source of pride and inspiration so as to make it more receptive to the problems of humanity and the issues of modernity, to make of the state the guardian of the sanctity of the tolerant values of Islam and its rational spirit of interpretation, to make mosques the houses of God alone lest they be turned into arenas for political conflict and pulpits that nurture the seeds of division.
- Tunisia's commitment to the Code of Personal Status and supplementary provisions, and the recognition of the reforms embodied therein and affecting family life and women's emancipation.

In addition to the Pact, the law on political parties has helped organize pluralism since its institution on May 3, 1988. It stipulates that each party should serve the values and principles of human rights, that it should defend the republican values and sovereignty of the people, and that it should guarantee the respect of the values incorporated in the Code of Personal Status, including women's freedom and children's rights.

Throughout all the above, there are references that purport to ban fanatic parties of a fundamentalist religious or other character that bring in the authority of theologians or the dictatorship of the proletariat to dismiss the sovereignty of the people.

The law on political parties also stipulates "the repudiation of violence in all its forms as well as extremism, of racial segregation, and all other forms of discrimination." No political party is entitled to base its principles or activities on religion, language, race, gender, or region. These are principles that Tunisia has adopted from international instruments of human rights.

It is on those grounds that the *Nahdha* Movement and the Communist Party of Tunisian Workers were banned, given that both of them reject republican values, use violence, and advocate fanaticism and extremism. We have already noted that the Tunisian Penal Code incriminates all acts of solicitation of hatred or racial and religious discrimination, treating all these as organized terrorism.

On that basis, partisans of those movements are prosecuted, because through affiliation, through action on behalf of these movements, by funding, distributing pamphlets, or attending their meetings, they lay the foundations of an extremist, fanatic ideology and encourage others to embrace it as the guiding philosophy of their actions.

That is why the incrimination of these movements has been received by our society with an unreserved welcome. It has also been the subject of a wide recognition by international circles, including human rights organizations. The most significant precedent is perhaps that related to Mr. Ahmed Kahlaoui, who was brought to trial in Tunisian courts for publishing a statement advocating the assassination of Jews. He was defended by the outlawed movements, the *Nahdha* and the Communist Party of Tunisian Workers, who filed the case to the United Nations Working Group on Arbitrary Detention. The Working Group, as we have seen in previous paragraphs, upheld the judgment of the Tunisian courts, deciding that his crime was not one of conscience, but a common law crime, and that the Tunisian courts were entitled to sanction such acts.

While the door was being closed on such movements, it was being opened to democratic opposition, and that is a difficult equation that requires a mastery of the mechanisms of political action. For how does one permit enough political liberalization for the benefit of the democratic opposition, without allowing extremist movements to swallow them up? The most indicative illustration of that political mastery is the succession of amendments brought since the Change to the electoral system in Tunisia.

Amendments to the Electoral System and Inherent Objectives

The electoral system has been subject to successive, detailed amendments, with implications that are not immediately apparent to the casual observer. However, there lies behind those amendments inherent objectives which must now be elucidated, whether they relate to the system of legislative elections or to that of municipal elections.

Starting with legislative elections, the system of proportional representation was discarded as it did not serve the interests of the still fragile democratic opposition. All it would have done in the elections of 1989 for example, would have been to make certain the victory of the Democratic Constitutional Rally by 79.75% of the votes, and to give the independent lists the opportunity to take the lead of the opposition with 13.63% of the votes, whereas the parties of the democratic opposition would have shared out only 6% of the vote. As we all know, the independent lists comprised a mixture of opposition candidates, essentially endorsed by extremists. Depending on electoral districts, the extremists were either Islamic fundamentalists (8%), or others.

The opposition parties adopted the line of defending proportional representation in the beginning. However, they soon retreated from that position, because, to my mind, the figures had convinced them of its danger to the electoral system, as well as the concomitant risk of marginalization it bore to democratic opposition and the supremacy it meant for non-democratic opposition.

Therefore, the majority system was maintained, with voting cast in one session, on the basis of lists, transferable votes, and the possibility of electoral representation of voters: The system did not achieve the desired objectives, as transfer was not used. The Democratic Constitutional Rally carried 79% of the vote, and all 141 seats in the Chamber of Deputies. There was an attempt for all the seven democratic opposition parties to stand on lists for a national consensus, but, for various reasons, the proposal never met with success.

The elections of April 2, 1989, had served as a barometer of the political weight of the different parties, and tested the new capabilities of the ruling party after the Change. Thus the electoral system served the function of identifying for the regime the potential of the democratic opposition for mobilization and competition with "the independent candidates," concealing extremist movements behind them.

The results of the 1989 elections were not without disappointment to the President of the Republic, since they did not reflect pluralism inside the Chamber of Deputies. Therefore, he gave his permission for a modernization of the electoral system that guarantees a presence of the democratic opposition in the Chamber.

On December 27, 1993, a new amendment was introduced to achieve the objectives previously described. Voting on the basis of lists was maintained, but the possibility of electoral representation was abolished, to reinforce the status of parties, move away from personalizing the elections, and preserve cohesion between candidates of the one party, even if its list was augmented by names from outside the party. Also, voting takes place by single ballot within electoral districts. The list with the majority of votes in the district wins all the seats allotted to that district. The remaining votes are not discarded, but counted for extra national representation, because the number of seats in the Chamber of Deputies is greater than the total number of seats allotted to electoral districts.

That is because a population quotient yields different results: 60,000 inhabitants per seat for electoral districts, and 52,500 per seat for the Chamber of Deputies. That means a total number of 163 seats for the Chamber of Deputies and a total number of seats of just 144 for electoral districts. The 19 seats making up the difference are distributed nationally on the basis of a common electoral factor, though independent lists cannot benefit from pooling votes across districts and it is therefore more difficult for them to win such seats.

Parties, however, may pool votes from all the districts where they did not win seats. Thus, they can win seats in proportion to the votes obtained in the various districts. The parties which obtain a minimum number of the votes are not excluded, as the minimum has been fixed at 3% of the votes of the electoral district to be able to claim back half the grant allocated for the campaign. In the elections of March 20, 1994, the system resulted in four of the democratic opposition parties winning 19 of the 163 seats (10 to the Socialist Democratic Movement, with 30,660 votes, 4 to the Renewal Movement, with 11,299 votes, 3 to the Unionist Democratic Union, with 9,152 votes, and 2 to the Popular Unity Party, with 8,391 votes).

The most important measure introduced by the last electoral amendment is the preference given to the candidates of the parties over candidates of the independent ballots. It did not prevent nomination outside recognized party lists, as other countries have done. That remains a sacred right for each citizen to exercise regardless of party affiliation. Nevertheless, party candidates enjoy the added advantage of being able to merge votes on a national level, whereas no independent lists standing in a particular electoral district are allowed to transfer votes nationally, as they have no candidates in other districts. That means the independent lists can stand in only one electoral district.

On the other hand, a party can nominate candidates for election in more than one district, and can therefore benefit from the transfer rule on the national level. If we keep in mind that the independent lists are usually the only route open for the nomination of extremist groups, then tipping the odds in favor of the democratic parties becomes understandable, as it is only that measure which keeps a tight rein on anti-democratic movements while giving a free hand to the democratic movements.

Opting for this way out shows the political leadership's sense of moderation in Tunisia, as it did not cut out independents even if extremists hide behind them, but favored the other candidates, thereby finding a balance between every citizen's right to nomination and every persuasion's right to co-exist, on the one hand, and society's right to promote those movements and policies it sees fit for the installation of a sound democratic model, on the other hand.

The rule preventing parties with less than 3% of the vote from claiming back half the grant allocated for the financing of electoral campaigns, as well as the cost of printing ballot papers, has a clear purpose. It aims to urge recent, fragile parties in the direction of coalition or unification. The forthcoming legislative elections may well see a change in that direction. Note that public funding for electoral campaigns is calculated on the basis of each thousand votes at the level of the electoral district.[120]

It is therefore no exaggeration on my part to say that Ben Ali's major worry, throughout the discussion of the electoral system bill, which I had direct experience of, was to buttress the democratic opposition by giving it space that was not available to the other competing lists.

It is perhaps the first time in the history of political systems that we see a ruling party amend an electoral system to benefit of the opposition. That may be unthinkable in well-established democracies, yet it is a reality in Tunisia that is installed in the pursuit of the way to pluralism and in the search for the means to prepare for the democratic alternative, to saturate the political arena with democrats, and to banish fundamentalists and movements of their ilk as far away as possible. That is basically Ben Ali's perspective, which represents the right way to establish pluralism in this critical transition period that supersedes the bygone one-party era.

Municipal elections have followed a gradual, balanced, and deliberate course. The system guarantees a comfortable majority inside the municipal council, on the one hand, and looks to foster the representation of other trends standing for the council, on the other hand. The code was modified on December 29, 1988, and on May 4, 1990. The proposals for amendments had the benefit of a consultation with the National Pact Supreme Council, in which all parties and political persuasions are represented.

The most important amendment in the municipal election system since 1990 is the awarding of half the seats to the first list past the post. The remaining vote is distributed across the other lists, including the list winning the first half in proportion to the number of seats obtained by each list, barring lists with less then 5%, which are not admitted.

In practice, the system means that independent candidates participate on an equal footing with the candidates of the parties, without advantage to any, on the grounds that municipal work does not require the sort of caution needed for legislative work. At any rate, the major deliberations of the council remain under the authority of local government. The small-size municipal district means that candidates will not be able to conceal any extremist tendencies they may have. In the elections of June 10, 1990, independent lists were able to win several of the municipality seats. Independents in the Chebba Municipality, including the candidates of the Communist Party of Tunisian Workers, managed to carry the majority of seats in the council and were surprised at the way the local authorities treated them and did not set them apart for belonging to a different party to the ruling one.

Former American Ambassador John McCarthy was delighted with the comments of the Mayor to the effect that the Municipal Council's relations with local government authorities were excellent, that he had received special encouragement from President Ben Ali himself, to the surprise of members of the council. After five years of being active on the Municipal Council, some of its members, including the Mayor, preferred to end their independent status to join the Democratic Constitutional Rally. In the elections of May 21, 1995, they stood for election on its lists.

Given the small size of some municipalities, a list may win the majority of seats, for example, with 251 votes in the Cherarda Municipality, with 262 votes in the Beni Mtir Municipality, or with 340 votes in the Chebika Municipality. Just 13 votes in Cherarda, 14 in Beni Mtir, or 17 in Chebika are enough to secure seats in the municipal council, to mention but a few examples.

However, opposition parties in the elections of May 21, 1995, were not sufficiently prepared and, to our mind, did not set for themselves a plan to focus on certain municipalities, according to their capacities. Consequently, their efforts were scattered, and they did not win a satisfactory share of the vote, particularly since coping with municipal elections takes its toll.

For example, the number of candidates nominated by each party reached a total of 4,074, in addition to 514 observers on the basis of two observers present at each ballot station. The Socialist Democratic Movement, which had decided to stand in all the municipalities, preferred in the end to stand on separate lists in just 23 municipalities. The Liberal Social Party stood only at Ksar Gafsa on an independent list. The Progressive Socialist Rally stood only at the Hammam Chott Municipality. Its list was legally inadmissible. The Renewal Movement, the Popular Unity Party, and the Unionist Democratic Union preferred to stand as a coalition in 16 municipalities. There were two other independent lists at Mahdia and Zeramdine.

The last municipal elections of May 21, 1995, were an opportunity to assess once again the status of democratic opposition. Some, like the troika of parties in the coalition, did display sound judgment, stating that the pluralist choice required a greater effort and stamina on the part of the opposition as much as on the part of the ruling party, for us to achieve the common objectives laid down since the Change, and the aspirations that Ben Ali inspires in all of us. On June 5, 1995, the Executive Committee of the Renewal Movement released a statement saying just that.[121] The Socialist Democratic Movement was alone in expressing irritation, perhaps because of its disappointment after the optimistic expectations it had pinned on the elections.

Ben Ali expressed disquiet at the results obtained, but did not lay the blame at anyone's door. In fact, I remember him emphasizing, in a meeting just days after the elections, the need for more thinking to seek other formulas to push pluralism forward, to create better and more favorable conditions for the democratic opposition, particularly by boosting its ability to carry out more effective campaigns to secure a meaningful representation in elected state institutions, local and central.

Independence...Indifference

The existence of independents needs to be analyzed in political systems in general, and in nascent democracies in particular. It may well be natural for some people to be indifferent to political life, to stay out of the contest by not joining a party or voting for one. Nevertheless, that trend takes on a worrying quality in nations which are on their way to pluralism, since they need a maximum of participation to give a real sense of competition, and to help curb the advance of extremism so as to bolster nascent democratic movements. As one opinion poll carried out by the Social Research Department (1993) revealed, 64% of those asked did not belong to any political party or association. The same survey shows the reason significantly (29%) to be "lack of information," that is, the lack of a tradition of collective action.

In one-party nations, political life is restricted to a few professionals, who live off the party and the state. Politics in such nations is a professional occupation, which concerns only a particular stratum of the population. The rest retire from political work, on the grounds that retirement, for conscientious elites, is a form of protest. They do not care for the one party, or for associations and organizations emanating from it or controlled by it. They do not take part in voting, do not read opinion papers, and do not follow the news. In short, they do not keep themselves informed of what goes on in political life, as if it were a select activity that concerned exclusively those who practise it. In fact, they only chat about the news of politicians' personal lives, and affairs of the seraglio, as the saying goes. Tunisia lived in the shadow of that situation before the Change, starting from the middle of the 1970s.

Indifference in public opinion breeds apathy toward political life, and more generally toward affairs of the state, causing an ingrained pattern of resigned, dazed disposition to be passed on from one generation to the next. That behavior characterizes the elites primarily, but also affects the man in the street. Such reservations increase the political vacuum that we have described above, because, besides the absence of democratic opposition, of voluntary social clubs for intellectual and practical pursuits, and of other institutions of civil society, the new regime finds in the majority of people, elites or not, a kind of resignation and aversion to political work, as the old regime had killed in them any motivation to participate or compete and had robbed them of any desire to serve the public good. A great many of them come to be afraid that entering political life might be interpreted as a Machiavellian, hypocritical move to pacify the regime.

That is why it was no easy task for the regime to reverse attitudes, to create a new climate for greater and greater participation in political life. And had it not been for people's trust and confidence, the regime would have faced real obstacles in its efforts to remove the mentality of withdrawal, fear, and escapism, and would have been unable to instill the desire to participate and compete in many of the social groups that came forward to support the Change, impelled by belief in its principles, by a sense of responsibility for its success, as well as by a conviction that working real change is a task that lies not so much in the hands of the state as it does in the hands of society as a whole.

Most of the elites have expressed loyalty to, and confidence in, Ben Ali, as well as belief in the integrity of the new policies, yet certain persons of national distinction remain reluctant to participate, still refusing to join in the new political dynamism, whether through party membership, party activities, or participation in political debates being played out on the pages of newspapers and other instruments of public opinion. They are people who still await a formal invitation to do so, or an official appointment in such capacities, without having to work for them through the existing party structures or institutions of civil society.

That logic is one of the vestiges of the old one-party regime, and as such needs time to disappear, and to be superseded by a predisposition for initiative, by the search to partake in shaping the political destiny of the community, by a commitment to a clear, specific line of action, and by hard work for that ideal and for its application and triumph, through the openings available to each and everyone whether in the institutions of the government or the opposition.

I still recall how some of those persons of distinction, despite allegiance to the project of the Change, refused to join the different existing parties, under the pretext that figures from the old regime were still there, or that certain personalities belonged to them who had rather left their mark on the history of the opposition in bygone days.

Thus, those figures preferred to remain outside the political arena, though still criticizing those parties for not getting rid of the symbols of the old regime. Ben Ali's answer was that it was up to them to take the initiative, and to join those parties and change things however they saw fit, and to the extent that they could muster.

That is because, rather than excluding anyone, Ben Ali insists on the creation of openings and motivation. Politics is a battle which calls upon professional figures of the Change who have missed the train to assume the full responsibility for it, to accept the need to work hard for the sake of putting their ideas into activist practice, and to carve for themselves the place they deserve.

The regime has made it its business to open up all opportunities for persons of high caliber, whatever fields of specializations or persuasions they may have. They in turn have continually turned up in great numbers to give the national debate substance, and to the national political project an intellectual essence. However, some of those persons still remain untouched by the fighting political spirit required for the Change. That is a spirit that is not acquired by diplomas, but by practice in the political field, inside parties and associations. Some still stand by, looking on, not opposed to what is going on, but not involved in the thick of things.

Democratic competition, we all know, requires the strongest participation possible, not just by the rank and file, but also by the elites. Moreover, in this era of competition being experienced by Tunisia today, he who does not participate leaves a vacuum. He who does not lead in the direction he wants finds himself pushed in the direction he does not want. Yet, in the struggle to fill the political vacuum, democracies in their infancy need the support of every single voice. They particularly need the high-profile elites capable of shaping public opinion, of winning over those who lack awareness to the democratic cause, and of influencing them to work within, not outside, the system and to subscribe to the sound social model at hand.

What is notable is that all elites, without exception whatsoever, took part in forcefully laying siege to extremist movements, each from his own position, from formal political fora, from university platforms, from cultural centers, from the rostra of public meetings, from narrow family circles, as well as on celebrations and other occasions.

Yet, some missed the opportunity to join in the democratic political platforms, whether inside the ruling party or inside the opposition. Efforts are now underway, particularly by the opposition but also by the ruling party, to focus on the activation, to use a current phrase, of that national talent. Those elites are for the policies installed by the Change, believe and trust in Ben Ali's project, and in his ability to secure a better future for Tunisia. They are there on major occasions, to lecture, engage in debate, vote and defend. But they have not joined the party structures and are still reticent about throwing all their weight and energy into organized, formal action.

I have in fact raised this issue because I believe that proactive participation is incumbent upon the elites, that the onus is on them to secure the road to pluralism. It is not enough that they should be content with what is going on or to champion the policies of the Change; they have to take part, within the dictates of their intellectual conviction, in the existing political contest. They are not independent, as they claim. Rather, at this historic moment of society's march, they have deserted. Ben Ali believes that the country is in dire need of all national talent, without any exception.

The way to pluralism is through the active participation of the elites, in order that the intellectual groundwork may be established for the national debate, that a leadership structure may be formed for political competition, that all Tunisians may be offered policies and alternatives as a basis for electoral comparison and choice.

In Tunisia, women have played a major role in vanguard action. They have managed to create a powerful dynamism in the ruling party, in the democratic opposition, in the National Union of Women, and in many of the associations of various trends. A dramatic indication of that dynamism is women's turnout at elections. In 1989, only 260,000 women took part in the elections. In 1994, thanks to an effective, continued mobilization, their participation leaped beyond one million.[122]

Their old battle now over, they have embarked on a fresh one. The old battle was that for equality with men, which has indeed been achieved, the law now free of anything that discriminates between men and women. The new battle lies in the struggle for participation, because women have come to realize that their achievements can only be safeguarded through actual involvement in all opportunities for debate and in positions of power. Women in Tunisia are a bastion against the fundamentalist movement, who have stood up to it ferociously as the real danger threatening their freedom and dignity, as well as the freedom and dignity of their sons and daughters.

That is why Tunisia has put her money on her women, bringing them into prominence, and encouraging them to be part of the decision-making process. Ben Ali has also made it clear in all his statements that Tunisia is committed to her liberal line of policy, that there is no going back on the achievements accomplished for the benefit of women and the family. In particular, he has stated that the major credit for defending against the fundamentalist movement was due to women's resistance and the fighting spirit that allowed them to defend their achievements, to muster enthusiasm, to show courage, and to excel even in the farther reaches of Tunisia in that defense.

On August 13, 1993, Ben Ali promulgated pioneering legislation that erected the second landmark in the history of women's emancipation, after the first landmark of 1956, which instituted the Code of Personal Status. The new legislation lays the foundations of a genuine complementarity between men and women, and of joint responsibility for child custody. In addition, new rights were acquired by women, including the right to pass on the woman's nationality to her underage children in case her husband is a foreigner. Tunisian women have hailed this right as a great source of pride in the homeland, since they are now, like men, able to pass on their nationality and with it the sense of patriotism and citizenship to their children.

If one wished to make comparisons with other nations on their way to pluralism, one would find that Algeria too is leading the battle against fundamentalist fanaticism with the participation of women. Theirs is indeed a heroic participation, one that has not gone unnoticed by analysts. One need only see the mass demonstrations staged by women in the streets of Algiers, the slogans they have shouted in the face of fanatic movements, and the summary trials to which they have brought the leaders of fundamentalism for the crimes they have perpetrated against Algerian society and against humanity.

Among other elites which have lent valuable support to the pluralist orientation in Tunisia are the journalists. The media played a vital role in exposing the double talk of the fundamentalists, and in alerting the public to the threat this movement poses to democracy. In Algeria, too, journalists engaged upon an activist mission, although their task was more difficult there, as efforts were not united in the struggle against fanaticism. Fifty newsmen and newswomen were killed, in an atrocious manner, because, to fundamentalists, they are the most important backers of the regime, and "he who puts the pen to fighting them, they will put the sword to his neck," as they put it.

The building stage of democracy does not admit any resignation, or shirking of responsibility. He who will not take a proactive, concrete part in boosting the democratic process, unbeknownst to himself contributes to boosting the anti-democratic momentum. □

CONCLUSION:
Pluralism...and Then?

BEN ALI HAS CHOSEN to embark on the road to pluralism, even though he could have maintained the then-prevalent one-party system. The threat of fundamentalism, compounded with the deteriorating social conditions at that time, could have been pretexts for an iron-handed policy and a postponement of liberalization. But Ben Ali preferred the road to pluralism, because of his personal conviction that it is the only way to protect society from discord and political crises. Pluralism affords the opportunity for different opinions to remain in contention, and for opposed interests to come to the surface, to be continually expressed in a public, peaceful manner. Pluralism also secures the participation of all national human resources in the building process—and how badly are nascent democracies in need of all the resources of their sons and daughters! Pluralism also reduces a regime's isolation—and how badly are such regimes in need of public support! Pluralism alone marginalizes extremism and promotes consensus.

However, Ben Ali's pluralist choice has far greater implications. For him, pluralism guarantees for Tunisia growing, effective prosperity, so much so that prosperity, in his eyes, cannot be real if not founded on freedom. The two are interdependent.

A free economy cannot evolve without political liberalization, and vice versa. That is why we see that the regime has called upon free initiative, has taken the state's hands off the economy, has eased the weight of bureaucracy to enable the administration to give an incentive to the transactions of individuals and institutions, not to be an obstacle to them. Anyone who has known Ben Ali closely knows that he is liberal by nature.

He has an aversion to advance authorizations, to administrative complications, and to protracted procedures. Therefore he made a point of reducing the number of economic transactions that require authorizations by almost 90%. Where authorizations were in force, he replaced them with the system of specifications, which frees institutions of any constraints except those they accept in the terms and conditions. Freedom for him is the rule, restraint the exception. The state has to focus on discharging its other duties, to see to it that competition takes place in all fairness, to lay standards for it, and to activate and motivate the processes of development.

There is a latent motive that has not been sufficiently developed in Ben Ali's public discourse, but that has always been there in his thinking. It is, to my mind, the most significant motive behind pluralism. That is the patriotic motive, Ben Ali's desire to kindle anew the feeling of patriotism, which in the old era was obviously on the wane.

Some might think this inference rather odd, that there is no direct link between pluralism and patriotism. Yet the pluralist orientation in Tunisia, which is only eight years old, has patently solidified the relationship between pluralism and patriotism. Observers can feel that a forceful, patriotic feeling has been restored to Tunisians, that the right to difference has generated a duty to preserve unity, that competing opinions and interests coalesce around a nobler ideal, that is the love, reverence, and exaltation of one's country. A Tunisian now feels that he is a real citizen, that his opinion is important, and that he has the right to express it and put it forward in national debates. Hence, he feels devotion and pride for belonging to Tunisia, happiness for her good fortune, sadness for her misfortune. That is a general feeling across the board, affecting the elites as well as the rank and file, whatever their social status or intellectual affiliation. The national consensus, as we say in Tunisia, now offers acceptance to all opinions and understanding to all interests, except for opinions that taint the sanctity of the homeland or harm the national interests of Tunisia.

One feels Ben Ali's outward pleasure at all those feelings, as he refers to them on every occasion. One also feels this in his special meetings with ambassadors or foreign journalists, as he lauds a member of the opposition who refrains from any criticism that may be derogatory or degrading of Tunisia. He has no time for Tunisians who do not reply vigorously, at international forums, to any unfair criticism, or any comment prejudicial to the national interests of Tunisia. One might say that Ben Ali rates people, in power or in the opposition, according to how much reverence they have for their country, according to how eager they are in defending Tunisia. He acknowledges the right of anyone, in the ruling party or outside it, to object, to assert a different opinion, whatever the content of that opinion. But he is averse to that opinion being expressed in any way that damages the national achievements, as if the reason for difference were not to make a constructive, critical contribution, but to sow suspicion and place obstacles. An example of that is Ben Ali's attitude toward organizations which do not proclaim their opinions in Tunisia, do not try to start a dialogue with the government, but quickly dash off faxes to foreign news agencies and to personalities and institutions outside Tunisia. Another example is his attitude to those who would disclose to ambassadors and foreign journalists what they would not declare, defend, or discuss openly in Tunisia.

I recall organizations which just would not quit or reform. They insisted on transmitting their positions to dubious foreign personalities, who undertook to publicize them and use them to defame and discredit the regime. We all recall also the candidate for the Presidency of the Republic in 1994, who, knowing full well that he was not eligible for election, instead of sending his candidacy to the proper committee, sent it to the French news agency.

Pluralism is the choice that has enabled democracies the world over to refine a number of common values that are not to be altered by competitors. The first of these values is the love of one's country and the defense of its interests, so that competition stops where the common interest of the country starts. Rarely do we hear a member of the opposition in Western democracies saying anything unfavorable to his country, and rarely do we find a member of the opposition in these democracies daring inside his country to maintain opinions or positions the majority of people regard as opposed to the priorities or interests of their country.

Undoubtedly, the absence of pluralism in many political systems of our region has generated non-democratic movements, under the pretext of a more encompassing pan-Arab or religious identity, whose partisans do not believe in the country concerned, but are carried away by broader ideologies and complicated alliances which seek, *inter alia*, to do damage to the interests of their own country, and to its values and achievements. Religious fundamentalist movements have not been patriotic ones, nor have pan-Arab movements.

Those ideologies serve neither Islam nor Arabism. Had they been truly Islamic or Arabist, there would not have been that many of them, and there would not have been any conflicts between them. In reality, they are contained movements devoted to individual leaders, who yearn to have a dominion beyond the boundaries of their own country. Some of them had a success of sorts, for a limited period; most of them, and they are many, failed to win supporters, even at a narrow, national level. I do not wish to mention them by name, but any skilled observer will know precisely who I mean.

Ben Ali's ideology then, I can safely say, is based in a broader sense on patriotism. That is not some kind of imperialist nationalism, but a sincere, true patriotism. It is not a form of hostility to others, but an affirmation of the Tunisian self. It does not seek isolation from the world, but an assertion of difference for the sake of a richer contribution.

It does not reject other cultures, but looks to participate in, and contribute to, a universal, human culture that promotes the belief that humanity can make no progress without the participation of all cultures.

It is the sort of patriotism based not on hegemony, but on partnership; not on a one-party state, but on a pluralist society. The ideology of patriotism, for Ben Ali, does not rely on imposing this orientation by force, but on preparing the ground for it by promoting freedom, acknowledging differences to foster consensus, congruity, harmony, and unity.

The way to pluralism, then, turns out to be the way to patriotism. We could easily rewrite the various parts of this book, and the discussion of Ben Ali's strategic trinity of challenges, with the description of the way to pluralism replaced by a description of the way to true patriotism. The elimination of the vacuum left behind by the previous one-party regime requires the development of all the trends that foster consensus in the midst of difference, and the establishment of institutions which place the interests of the nation above the different interests of individuals. Also, to kindle the patriotic spirit is to banish fundamentalist and extremist left-wing movements, which believe not in nationhood, but in expansionist movements in the name of supremacy for the Islamic Umma or for the international proletariat.

Those movements did not originate in Tunisia, did not grow on Tunisian soil, but were and still are ideologically, organizationally, and financially tied to foreign governments and forces, standing at their beck and call and dedicated to their interests. To kindle the patriotic spirit we must involve everybody, and open the forums of pluralist, civil society to a wider and deeper dialogue. We must change our educational system to raise our children on other values than those that had slipped in, in decades past.

We conclude by saying that Ben Ali would like for the new climate he has founded for Tunisia to restore confidence and optimism in the future. He wants peace, security, freedom, and justice, and the creation of the appropriate climate for motivation and participation, that all Tunisia's sons and daughters might take part in restoring her to her former glory, which spans 3,000 years of history, and to her former standing and vital role in the Mediterranean region, through which she was able to enrich universal culture throughout the ages. Pluralism is not an end in itself, but a means. Filling the vacuum left behind by the previous one-party era is the real building block, with which we can lay the foundations of a durable prosperity, and preserve Tunisia's integrity with a moderate society, where difference leads to harmony, and dialogue to consensus, a society that thus is able to banish all forms of fanaticism and extremism, and all imported ideologies, so that finally there is only one way left, that is pluralism, and one ideology, that is a patriotism reserved for Tunisia, and nothing else but Tunisia. □

BIBLIOGRAPHY
Excerpts Cited From President Ben Ali's Addresses

Excerpt from Ben Ali's address on November 7, 1987.
Excerpt from Ben Ali's address on July 25, 1987.
Excerpt from Ben Ali's address on February 3, 1988
Excerpt from Ben Ali's address on March 31, 1988.
Excerpt from Ben Ali's address on May 1, 1988.
Excerpt from Ben Ali's address on May 25, 1988 (in Addis Ababa).
Excerpt from Ben Ali's address on July 1, 1988 (in Carthage).
Excerpt from Ben Ali's address on July 29, 1988.
Excerpt from Ben Ali's address on July 31, 1988.
Excerpt from Ben Ali's address on November 3, 1988.
Excerpt from Ben Ali's address on November 7, 1988.
Excerpt from Ben Ali's address on July 10, 1989.
Excerpt from Ben Ali's address on November 7, 1989.
Excerpt from Ben Ali's address on May 1, 1990.
Excerpt from Ben Ali's address on July 12, 1990.
Excerpt from Ben Ali's address on April 9, 1991.
Excerpt from Ben Ali's address on July 17, 1991 (Science Day).
Excerpt from Ben Ali's address on November 2, 1992 (in Carthage).

Works Cited

A group of authors, *L'Algérie aujourd'hui,* Paris, Ed. Paris Plus, 1992.

A group of authors, *Le changement politique au Maghreb,* Paris, CNRS, 1991.

Al-Ahmadi, Abdallah, *Human Rights and Public Liberties in Tunisian Law* (in Arabic), Tunis, Orbis Impression, 1993.

Al-Basyouni, Mahmoud Sharif, *Human Rights* (Two volumes), Beirut, Dar Al-'Ilm Lil-Malayin, 1989.

Al-Fitouhi, Wafa Al-Khalifi, *The Progressive Socialist Rally and the Unionist Democratic Union* (in Arabic), Postgraduate Research Project, Tunis, Faculté de Droit, 1995.

Allani, Alya, *The Movement of the Islamic Tendency in Tunisia (1970-1987)* (in Arabic), Tunis, The Faculty of Humanities and Social Sciences, 1993.

Allonache, Merzek and **Colonna, Vincent,** *Algérie 30 ans. Les enfants de l'indépendance,* Paris, Ed. Autrement, 1992.

Al-Ma'arifa, Edition No. 4, Volume V. .

Almond, Gabriel and **Powell, Bingham,** *Comparative Politics. A Developmental Approach,* 1966 (Translated into French; in the series: Tendances Actuelles, 1972).

Almond, Gabriel and **Verba, Sydney,** *The Civic Culture. Political Attitudes and Democratic Nations,* Princeton, 1963.

As-Sahafa, August 12, 1994.

Amami, Abdallah, *The Nahdha Movement, Terrorist Organizations in the Islamic World: The Nahdha Model* (in Arabic), Tunis, STD, 1992.

Amnesty International, "An Integrated Strategic Plan," London, December 1994 (Internal Document).

Anderson, Lisa, "Politics and democracy," in *Government and opposition,* 1990.

Apter, David, *The Politics of Modernization,* 1965.

Association Tunisienne de Droit Pénal, *L'instruction,* Seminar Proceedings, Manuscript, Tunis, 1992.

ATCE, "Rached Ghannouchi: The Face and the Mask," Tunis, Publications of the Agency of External Communications (ATCE), 1992.

Attali, Jacques, *Les modèles politiques,* Paris, PUF, 1992.

Badie, Bertrand, "Démocratie et religion," in UNESCO, *Repenser la démocratie,* RISS, August 1991.

Balta, Paul, *Islam, civilisations et sociétés,* Paris, Ed. Rocher, 1991.

Balta, Paul, *L'Islam et le monde,* Paris, Coll. La Mémoire du Monde, 1991.

Barrour, Emmy, in **Gresh, Alain** (ed.), *A l'Est, des nationalismes contre la démocratie),* op. cit. p. 114.

Bel Haj Hammouda, Ajmi, "Le silence de l'inculpé," in Association Tunisienne de Droit Pénal, *L'instruction,* Seminar Proceedings, Manuscript, Tunis, 1992.

Ben Achour, Iyadh, "Islam et Laicité," in *Revue Pouvoirs,* No. 62, 1992, pp. 15-31.

Ben Achour, Rafi', "Verification of the constitutionality of laws" (in Arabic), in *Mélanges Mzioudet,* Tunis, Faculté de Droit, 1994, pp. 82-7.

Ben Fdhila, Fatma, and **Labidi, Najiba,** *The Islamic Movement in Tunisia: The single objective and the double talk* (in Arabic), Tunis, The Institute of Journalism, 1990.

Ben Hamda, Abdelmajid, "Religious Achievements in Tunisia the New Era" in joint work with **Chaabane, Sadok,** *November 7, A quiet revolution* (in Arabic), Abdulkarim Ben Abdallah Publishing, 1992.

Ben Jaballah, Hamadi, "Educational reform and the human values epic," in joint work with **Chaabane, Sadok,,** *November 7, A quiet revolution* (in Arabic), Abdulkarim Ben Abdallah Publishing, 1992.

Ben Miled, Slim, *La présidence à vie de la république,* Tunis, Faculté de Droit, 1985.

Ben Youssef Charfi, Salwa, *La Ligue Tunisienne pour la Défense des Droits de l'Homme,* Faculté de Droit, 1987.

Berstein, Serge, *Démocratie, Régimes autoritaires et totalitarismes au 20è siècle,* Paris, Hachette, 1994.

Berteji, Brahim, *La gratuité de la justice,* Tunis, Faculté de Droit, 1989.

Bibo, Istvan, *Misère des petits Etats de l'Europe de l'Est,* Paris, A. Michel, 1993 (Trans.).

Blibech, Fadhel, *Les associations,* Tunis, Faculté de Droit, 1993.

Bruckner, Pascal, *La mélancolie démocratique,* Paris, Seuil, 1990.

Camau, Michel, *Pouvoirs et institutions au Maghreb,* Tunis, CERES Productions, 1978.

Chaabane, Sadok, *Analyse stratégiste des processus de gouvernement dans les sociétés en transition,* Tunis, Faculté de Droit, 1975.

Chaabane, Sadok, *The Democracy of Consensus, in* The Democratic Constitutional Rally, *Democratic Changes in the World Today* (an international symposium), 1988.

Chaker, Mustapha, *Histoire du Parti Communiste Tunisien,* Postgraduate Research Project, Paris, 1972.

114

Charfi, Abdelmajid, *Islam and Modernism* (in Arabic), Tunis, STD, 1991.

Colas, Dominique, *Le glaive et le fléau, Généalogie du fanatisme et de la société civile,* Paris, Grasset, 1992.

Crozier, Michel, *La société bloquée,* Paris, 1987.

Dahl, Robert, "A preface to democratic theory," Chicago, 1956.

Dahl, Robert, *L'avenir de l'opposition dans les démocraties* (Trans.), Paris, Laffont, 1966.

Dahl, Robert, *Modern Political Analysis, 1963* (Trans. *L'analyse politique contemporaine,* Paris, Laffont, 1973).

Deutsh, Karl, *The Nerves of Government. Models of Political Communication and Control,* New York, 1963

Diamond, Linz J. and **Lipset, S.,** *Les pays en développement et l'expérience de la démocratie,* Paris, Nouveaux Horizons, 1993, pp. 23-30.

Duhamel, Olivier, *Les Démocraties,* Paris, Seuil, 1993.

Dunn, Michael Collins, *Political Islam: The Case of Tunisia's al-Nahda,* Washington, The International Estimate, 1992, p. 105.

Easton, David, *A System Analysis of Political Life,* New York, 1965 (Trans. *Analyse systématique de la vie politique,* Paris, A. Colin, 1971).

Elleinstein, Jean, *D'une Russie à l'autre. Vie et mort de l'URSS,* Paris, Messidor, 1992, pp. 723-730.

Fukuyama, F., *La Fin de l'Histoire et le Dernier Homme,* Paris, Flammarion, 1992.

Ga'loul, Mtir, *Guarantees of the Supremacy of the Constitution in Tunisia* (in Arabic), Tunis, Faculté de Droit, 1994.

Gaxie, Daniel, *Les professionnels de la politique,* Paris, PuF, 1973.

Gratchen, Andrei, "Réfléchir à l'expérience soviétique," in Alain Gresh (ed.), *A l'Est, les nationalismes contre la démocratie,* Paris, Edition Complexe, 1993, p. 83.

Gresh, Alain (ed.), *A l'Est, des nationalismes contre la démocratie,* Paris, Edition Complexe, 1993.

Guéhenno, Marie, *La fin de la démocratie,* Paris, Flammarion, 1993.

Guy Hermet in **Bidet, Jacques,** *Les paradigmes de la démocratie,* Paris, PUF, 1994.

Hermet, Guy, "Culture et démocratie," UNESCO, 1993.

Hermet, Guy, "Présentation: Le temps de la démocratie?", UNESCO, RISS, p. 267.

Hobsbawn(m), Eric, *Nations et nationalismes depuis 1789,* Paris, Gallimard, 1992.

Holt, R, and **Turner, J.,** *The Political Basis of Economic Development: An Exploration in Comparative Political Analysis,* Trans. in Tendances Actuelles, Paris, 1970.

Huntington, Samuel, *Political order in changing society,* New Haven, Yale University Press, 1968.

Huntington, Samuel. P., "The Clash of Civilizations," in *Foreign Affairs,* Summer 1993.

Ilchman, W. and **Uphoff,** in *Le changement politique à la lumière de l'analyse économique* (*Political Change in the Light of Economic Analysis*) (Trans.), Paris, Tendances Actuelles, 1975.

J'idane, Riydh, "The Teaching of Human Rights in Tunisia," published in the *Human Rights Magazine,* The International Institute of Human Rights, Strasbourg, France.

Jazi, Dali, *Les rapports entre l'Etat et le citoyen dans la Tunisie indépendante,* Ph.D. Thesis, Paris II, 1982.

Jeaît, Hichem, in Collective Work, *Islam et politique au Proche Orient aujourd'hui,* Paris, Gallimard, 1991.

Jeune Afrique Economique, "Les islamistes à l'assaut de l'Afrique Noire", No. 185, November 1994, pp. 101-109.

Jeune Afrique, "Ghannouchi: ce qui'il a dit à la police," No. 1396, October 7, 1987.

Jourshi, Salah Eddine, *The Islamic Movement in the Vortex* (in Arabic), Tunis, Dar al-Barraq, 1985.

Karl, Terry Lynn, and **Schmitter, Philippe,** "Les modes de transition en Amérique Latine," in UNESCO, *Le temps des démocraties en Europe du Sud et de L'Est,* RISS, No.128, April 1991, pp. 285-302.

Keddie, Nikki R. "The Islamist Movement in Tunisia," in *Maghreb Review,* Vol. 11, No. 1, 1986.

Kefi, Faiza, *Le droit à l'éducation et l'enseignement des droits de l'homme,* Tunis, ATCE, 1992.

Kirkpatrick, Jeane, "Dictatorships and Double Standards," in *Commentary,* 68 (November, 1979), pp. 34-35.

La Republica.

Lamhichi, Abderrahim, *Islam et contestation au Maghreb,* Tunis, 1989.

Les étapes de la croissance politique, 1975. (French Trans.)

Les temps modernes, "Algérie, la guerre des frères," numéro spécial, January 1995.

Lijphar, Arend, "Théorie et pratique de la loi de la majorité: La tenacité d'un paradigme imparfait," in UNESCO, RISS, *Repenser la démocratie,* August, 1991, pp. 515-527.

Lipset, Seymour Martin, *Political Man,* Baltimore, John Hopkins University Press, 1981.

Ltayef, Mondher, *Presidency of the Republic in Tunisia* (in Arabic), Tunis, Faculté de Droit, 1993.

Ltayef, Shokri, *Islamists and Women: The Oppression Project* (in Arabic), Bayram Publishing, Tunis, 1988.

Lugau, Bernard, *Afrique (Africa),* Paris, Ed. Christian de Barbillat, 1975.

M'daffar, Zouheir, *Constitutional Law and Political Institutions,* Tunis, The Research Centre at the National School of Administration, 1992.

M'daffar, Zouheir, *Le Conseil Constitutionnel Tunisien,* Toulouse, Presses de l'IEP, 1995.

Mayer, N. and **Perrineau, P.,** *Les comportements politiques,* Paris, A. Colin, 1992.

Menyahan, John. A., *Learning Democracy, Memoirs of a University Lecturer* (in Trans.), Amman, Dar Al-Bashir, 1993.

Ming, Alain, *La vengeance des nations,* Paris, Grasset, 1990.

Moore, Henry Clement, *Tunisia Since Independence,* 1965.

Nguema, Issac, "Violences, Droits de l'homme et développement en Afrique," in *Revue Juridique et Politique, Indépendance et Coopération,* May, 1995, pp. 121-132.

Omar, Abdelfattah, *A Compendium of Constitutional Law* (in Arabic), Tunis, The Centre for Studies, Research, and Publication, 1987.

Percheron, Annick, *La socialisation politique,* Paris, A. Colin, 1993.

Pouvoirs, Volume I, *L'alternance,* 1977.

Pye, L. and **Verba, S.** (ed.) *Political culture and political development,* Princeton, 1965.

Rojzman, Charles, *La peur, la haine, et la démocratie,* Paris, Desclée de Brouwer, 1992.

Rosenbaum, A., *Political Culture,* New York, 1975.

Rostow, Walt, *The Stages of Economic Growth,* Cambridge, 1960.

Rupnik, Jacques, "L'invention démocratique en Europe du Centre-Est," in Minket Szurek (ed.), op. cit., p. 51; "Elections fondatrices," p. 56.

Rustow, Dankwart A., "Democracy: A global revolution?" in *Foreign Affairs,* 69: 4 (Autumn 1990), pp. 75-90.

Sarsar, M. Chéfik, *Le cadre juridique des partis politiques en Tunisie,* Postgraduate Research Project, Faculté de Droit, Tunis, 1990.

Sartori, Giovanni, *Parties and Party Systems,* Cambridge, Cambridge University Press, 1976.

Schartzenberg, R. G., *Sociologie politique,* Paris, Montchrétien, 1978.

Seiler, D. L., *Les partis politiques,* Paris, A. Colin, 1993.

Shils, E., *Political Development in the New States,* The Hague, Reed, 1965.

Tarchouna, Lotfi, "L'institution du médiateur administratif en Tunisie," in *Mélanges Mzioudet,* Tunis, Orbis Impression, 1994, pp. 291-325.

The Centre for Studies, Research, Documentation, and Information, "Women of Tunisia. Reality and Prospects" (in Arabic), Tunis, 1995.

The Democratic Constitutional Rally, summer school, 1994.

The High Commission for Human Rights, *The Annual Report on Human Rights in Tunisia* (in Arabic), Tunis, 1992.

The Renewal Movement, *Statement of June 5, 1995.*

The Sunday Express, *"Article,"* August 2, 1995.

Touati, Amine, *Algérie. Les Islamistes à l'assaut du pouvoir,* Paris, L'Harmattan, 1994.

Touraine, Alain, *Qu'est ce que la démocratie?* Paris, Fayard, 1994.

UNESCO, *Le temps de la démocratie,* RISS, No. 128, May 1991.

United Nations Publication, "United Nations Work in the Field of Human Rights."

Weffort, Fransisco, "Les démocraties nouvelles, Analyse du phénomène," in UNESCO, *La sociologie politique comparative,* RISS, No.136, March 1993.

Zartman, William, "La conduite de la réforme politique: le chemin de la démocratie," in *Tunisie: la politique économique de la réforme,* Tunis, Alif, 1995, pp. 22-45.

Zine, Mohamed, *Les droits de l'homme et les garanties de l'accusé dans le droit pénal,* Tunis, ATCE, 1992.

Laws, Regulations, Reports, and Conferences Cited

Act No. 1020/86, dated September 9, 1986, supplementing the French Penal Code, and **Act No. 541/87,** dated July 16, 1987 (France).

Act No. 399/99, dated August 27, 1986, and *its amendments* (USA).

Act No. 97 of 1992 (Egypt).

Basic Constitutional Law No. 32 of 1988, dated May 3, 1988, on the Organization of Political Parties.

Circulars No. 895 (December 16, 1991), **No. 904** (December 24, 1991), and **Decree No. 03/92,** dated September 30, 1992 (Algeria).

Law No. 112 of 1993, dated November 22, 1993, as a Supplement to the Penal Code, *Some Provisions of the Penal Code On the Incrimination of Hatred and Fanaticism.*

Law No. 113 of 1993, dated November 22, 1993, as an Amendment and Supplement to Certain Articles of the Code of Penal Procedures, *Some Provisions of the Penal Code On the Incrimination of Hatred and Fanaticism.*

Law No. 114 of 1993, dated November 22, 1993, as an Amendment and Supplement to Certain Articles of the Code of Penal Procedures, *Some Provisions of the Penal Code On the Incrimination of Hatred and Fanaticism.*

Law of June 18, 1993 (Switzerland).

No. 72 (February 24, 1992), by The Minister of the Interior.

The April 28, 1990 Act on the Constitutional Council's legislative competence.

The Code of the Press amendment of August 2, 1993 (Article 44).

The Emergency Act on Northern Ireland of 1991 (Britain).

The International Convention on Political and Civil Rights (Articles 12, 18, 19, 21, 22, 25, 26 and 27).

The Law of December 18, 1992, on the creation of the portfolio of Commissioner for Administration, or Ombudsman.

The Legislative Electoral System, amendment of December 27, 1993.

The Municipal Electoral Code, amendments of December 29, 1988, and of May 4, 1990.

The National Pact, signed on November 7, 1988.

The Ninth United Nations Conference on the Prevention of Crime in Cairo, *Egypt's proposal on relations between terrorism and organized crime (A/CONF/169L.12/ Rev1),* April 29 to May 8, 1995.

The Ninth United Nations Conference on the Prevention of Crime in Cairo, April 1995

The Penal Code, amendment of November 22, 1993.

The Regional Africa Convention held in preparation for the International Conference of Human Rights, *Tunis Declaration,* November 2-6, 1992.

The Tunisian Constitution, amendment of July, 1995, on the mandate of the Council.

The Tunisian Constitution, Article 2 on referendums.

The United Nations Code of Conduct for Law Enforcement Officers.

The United Nations Conference on Organized Crime in Napoli, Italy, November 21, 1994.

The United Nations Working Group on Arbitrary Detention, *Paragraphs from the Decision No. 12/1994 (TUNISIA),* dated September 28, 1994.

The Universal Declaration of Human Rights (Articles 7, 13, 14, 18, 19, 20, and 21).

The Vienna International Conference on Human Rights, *The Declaration and Agenda, June 14-25, 1993.*

Tunisia's Code of Personal Statute and supplementary provisions.

Tunisia's Code of Personal Statute, 1956.

Tunisia's Code of Personal Statute, amendment of August 13, 1993, on joint responsibility for child custody and women's right to pass on their nationality to their underage children if their husband is a foreigner.

Tunisian National Trade Union and the Tunisian Government, *Framework Agreement* on April 17, 1990.

United Nations Development Program, *Liberty of Human Development,* Report on Human Development 1990.

United Nations Development Program, *TUNISIA, Basic Initiatives in favor of Equality of the Sexes before the Law,* Report on Human Development 1995 (Sources: CAWTAR 1994, CREDIF and Tunisia 1994).

United Nations Development Program, *TUNISIA, Evolution of Human Development Indicator (HDI) in time: Ranking and Values for 1970 and 1992,* Report on Human Development 1995.

United Nations General Assembly, *Resolution No. 49/185 on human rights and terrorism,* December 23, 1994.

United Nations General Assembly, *Resolution No. 49/147, on the provisions and measures required for the prevention of all modern forms of racial discrimination and segregation, and of attendant fanaticism and intolerance,* December 23, 1994.

United Nations General Assembly, *Resolution No. 49/188, on the elimination of all forms of religious intolerance,* December 23, 1994.

United Nations General Assembly, *Resolution No. 49/213 on the United Nations Convention on Tolerance,* December 23, 1994. □

FOOTNOTES:

[1]On theories of political change see **Easton, David**, *A System Analysis of Political Life*, New York, 1965 (Trans. *Analyse systématique de la vie politique*, Paris, A. Colin, 1971). Easton links the evolution of a political regime to its external determinants. We have adopted this approach to some extent in our study of overflow control in the wake of the Change. Also **Huntington, Samuel**, *Political Order in Changing Society*, New Haven, Yale University Press, 1968. Huntington stresses the relation between the progress and functions of institutions and changes in society's character. **Shils, E**, *Political Development in the New States*, The Hague, Reed, 1965. Shils focuses on specialization of function, classifying regimes according to that criterion, the highest being political democracy. There is also a school that links economic development to political evolution, and confines democracy to societies with a high degree of economic development, including **Rostow, Walt**, *The Stages of Economic Growth*, Cambridge, 1960, and French translation of a book on *Les étapes de la croissance politique* (*Stages of Political Development*), 1975. Also see **Almond, Gabriel** and **Powell, Bingham,** *Comparative politics. A developmental approach*, 1966 (translated into French, in the series Tendances Actuelles, 1972). This latter theory compares political regimes according to their institutional ability to discharge specific functions vital to a political regime's life (the discrimination, expression, and reconciliation of different interests; the proclamation, implementation and follow-up of legislation).

There are other approaches to the study of political regimes which stress their ability to change economic and social conditions: **Apter, David,** *The Politics of Modernization*, 1965; or their ability to control and channel variables to serve their major objectives, on the basis of available information and means: **Deutsh, Karl,** *The nerves of government. Models of Political Communication and Control*, New York, 1963.

[2]One of the most outstanding studies devoted to Tunisia's approach to change and following a similar line of argument to our analysis is that by **Zartman, William,** "La conduite de la réforme politique: le chemin de la démocratie" ("The Conduct of Political Reform: The Way to Democracy"), in *Tunisie: la politique économique de la réforme* (*Tunisia: Economic Reform Policy*), Tunis, Alif, 1995, pp. 22-45. See also **Camau, Michel,** *Pouvoirs et institutions au Maghreb* (*Power and Institutions in the Maghreb*), Tunis, CERES Productions, 1978. **A group of authors,** *Le changement politique au Maghreb* (*Political Change in the Maghreb*), Paris, CNRS, 1991. The authors present an application of theories of political change to political regimes in the Arab Maghreb.

[3]See Robert Dahl's excellent study of the role of consensus in the development of democracy: **Dahl, Robert,** *Modern Political Analysis,* 1963 (Trans. L'analyse politique contemporaine, Paris, Laffont, 1973). On the specific role and advantages of consensus in the administration of democratic societies over the majority criterion, see also: **Lijphar, Arend,** "Théorie et pratique de la loi de la majorité: La tenacité d'un paradigme imparfait," ("Theory and Practice of the Majority Rule: the Persistence of an Imperfect Paradigm") in **UNESCO, RISS,** *Repenser la démocratie (Rethinking democracy),* August 1991, pp. 515-527. Prior to that work, the Democratic Constitutional Rally had already, in the first international symposium on "Democratic Changes in the World Today," 1988, devoted a study to precisely that issue: **Chaabane, Sadok,** *The Democracy of Consensus* (Arabic *dimuqratiyya al-wifaq*), which describes how the National Pact played a vital role in speeding up the creation of a consensus between the competing protagonists, and in preparing the ground for political democracy.

[4]**Zartman,** *op. cit.* (see footnote 2), says, "Neither the government nor the opposition knows what legitimate opposition means or how it should behave." He adds, "The transition from unilateralism to pluralism is a hot period in the history of every nation" (p. 23). See also: **Almond, Gabriel** and **Verba, Sydney,** *The Civic Culture. Political Attitudes and Democratic Nations,* Princeton, 1963, which distinguishes in particular a nonparticipative from a participative political culture.

[5]In this analysis, we use David Easton's theory, *op. cit.*, to elucidate the new regime's ability to control the social and political spurts concomitant with the Change.

[6]One of the most important references here is: **Fukuyama, F,** *La Fin de l'Histoire et le Dernier Homme (The End of History and the Last Man),* Paris, Flammarion, 1992, who regards liberal democracy as the ultimate stage of the ideological evolution of humanity and the final form of any human government (p. 11). Others argue that the triumph and spread of liberal democracy throughout the world will weaken it in the West, as it will not find voices to compete with and criticize it, thus losing the basis of a pluralist system: **Bruckner, Pascal,** *La mélancolie démocratique (The Melancholy of Democracy),* Paris, Seuil, 1990. For the different views on the collapse of communism and its effects on the ebb of democracy, see: **Guéhenno, Marie,** *La fin de la démocratie (The End of Democracy),* Paris, Flammarion, 1993, who argues that the movement of capital and people will result in the accumulation of power in the hands of specific international networks, leading to the disappearance of national boundaries and the dissipation of formal power.

[7]For a review of the main views on the subject, see: **Elleinstein, Jean,** *D'une Russie à l'autre. Vie et mort de l'URSS (From One Russia to the Other. The Life and Death of the USSR),* Paris, Messidor, 1992, pp. 723-730.

[8]There is support for this view in a number of studies: **Gresh, Alain** (ed.), *A l'Est, des nationalismes contre la démocratie (The East, on nationalism against democracy),* Paris, Edition Complexe, 1993. Also: **Hobsbawm, Eric,** *Nations et nationalism depuis 1789 (Nations and nationalism since 1789),* Paris, Gallimard, 1992. See also: **Rojzman, Charles,** *La peur, la haine, et la démocratie (Fear, Hatred, and Democracy),* Paris, Desclée de Brouwer, 1992; and **Ming, Alain,** *La vengeance des nations (The Revenge of Nations),* Paris, Grasset, 1990.

[9]Among the new theses advocating that line, which was later the object of criticism by several other analysts, is that by **Huntington, Samuel. P. ,** "The Clash of Civilizations," in *Foreign Affairs,* Summer 1993.

[10]He is a former spokesman for Gorbachev. see **Gratchen, Andrei,** "Réfléchir à l'expérience soviétique," ("Reflections on the Soviet Experience") in **Alain Gresh** (ed.),

A l'Est, les nationalismes contre la démocratie (*The East, on Nationalism against Democracy*), Paris, Edition Complexe, 1993, p. 83.

[11] See **Hobsbawm, Eric**, *Nations et nationalismes depuis 1789*, Paris, Gllimard, 1992. On the appearance of racism, see **Colas, Dominique**, *Le glaive et le fléau, Généalogie du fanatisme et de la société civile*, Paris, Grasset, 1992. A well-known Hungarian thinker has characterized ethnic or religious ideology as the ideology of hysteria: **Bibo, Istvan**, *Misère des petits Etats de l'Europe de l'Est*, Paris, A. Michel, 1993 (translation).

[12] In his November 2, 1992, address, President Ben Ali said, "There can be no democracy or a future for human rights while the doors are left open to terrorism, violence, and ethnic or religious extremism, which all hide behind human rights to emerge and expand, offering society a closed program that rejects difference and open-mindedness in the name of particularism and tradition."

[13] On March 28, 1995, German authorities arrested a Tunisian man named Abderrazak Arroum. In his house, they discovered weapons and explosives, as well as a number of blank Tunisian passports ready for forgery. It transpired that he was a member of "The Kindness Society," an Islamic charity (!) organization which is based in Zaghreb, and undertakes the recruitment and training of young members in Pakistan, Afghanistan and Bosnia, before returning them to their countries. It also transpired that the society had the patronage of the UN High Commission for Refugees, which was unaware of its secrets.

[14] Extremist movements have begun to set up bogus associations for the defense of human rights, with the aim of showering well-known non-governmental organizations, United Nations organizations, and eminent figures in the Western world (Members of Parliament, influential journalists, party leaders, etc.) with a flood of faxes on alleged human rights abuses or on real events, exaggerated all out of proportion. For that purpose, they have even made use of forged letters. See, for example, how specific persons (Ali Saidi, Mondher Sfar, and Ahmed Manai) set up certain organizations in France to defend fundamentalists in Tunisia, of which most had the same headquarters and common telephone and fax numbers, or in some cases no telephone or fax numbers. They include: Comité de Lutte contre la Répression, la Torture et pour les Libertés Publiques en Tunisie (The Committee for the Struggle against Repression and Torture, and for Public Liberties in Tunisia); Association Arabe des Droits de l'Homme (the Arab Association for Human Rights); Le Comité de Soutien à la Ligue des Droits de l'Homme (The Support Committee for the League of Human Rights); Collectif des Communautés Tunisiennes en Europe (The Collective for Tunisian Communities in Europe); and also: L'Union pour la Démocratie en Tunisie (The Union for Democracy in Tunisia), La Coordination pour la Défense des Libertés en Tunisie (Coordination for the Defense of Liberties in Tunisia); Le Conseil de la Communauté Tunisienne en France (The Council of the Tunisian Community in France); L'Union des Immigrés d'Eureux (The Union of the Immigrants of Eureux); L'Amicale des Tunisiens d'Eureux (The Society of Tunisians of Eureux); Comité de Soutien aux Victimes de la Répression en Tunisie (The Support Committee for the Victims of Repression in Tunisia).

[15] See **Amnesty International**, "An Integrated Strategic Plan," London, December 1994 (internal document).

[16] In his May 25, 1988 address in Addis Ababa, President Ben Ali said, "One strange paradox is the double standard used by those that would defend human rights...They turn a blind eye to the abuses their allies and friends commit in Africa or Asia, as if man in Africa, Asia, or in Namibia or·Palestine were not like man in the West or the East,

as if human rights were not utterly indivisible, not a common right to all humanity, without distinction or discrimination." See Also: **Kirkpatrick, Jeane,** "Dictatorships and Double Standards," *Commentary,* 68 (November, 1979), pp. 34-35.

[17]On August 2, 1995, Britain's *The Sunday Express* wrote, "After the investigations it has carried out, *The Sunday Express* is today in a position to reveal the disgraceful deal that permitted Rached Ghannouchi to lead a comfortable life in a country whose citizens he had tried to kill without mercy." The paper noted that it had become known that relations between Ghannouchi and major extremist Islamic groups based in the Middle East are a source of great anxiety for Western intelligence. Ghannouchi, the leader of the fundamentalist Tunisian movement known as "the *Nahdha,*" entertains close ties with the Islamic Salvation Front (the FIS). His arrival in Britain is sure to have aroused not only fear in his victims but also bewilderment. Labor MP Georges Poulkes has made a strong protest to the Home Office Minister, Michael Howard, for allowing Ghannouchi to live in Britain. The MP made a statement to the effect that that man should not have been permitted at all to enter the country oficially, that some of his victims live in this country, that that same man had maimed Helen Strochi physically and psychologically, as he has destroyed the rest of her life, that her friend, Alice Wright, who was 33 years of age and living in Ayrshire, still had memories of the evening she spent at the Sahara Beach Hotel and was distressed at the news that the man responsible for the attack was enjoying a cozy life in Britain instead of being behind prison bars, and that she wanted a convincing reply from the head of MI5 or MI6. She added, "It's a travesty. He should have been in prison, so why was he allowed to live in this country after all he has done? Why do we offer our protection to someone like that? Who can then guarantee he will not commit the same base acts again?"

The third victim was a working woman of 33 years of age, who was so terrified by the incident that she asked not to be identified for fear she might be the target of other attacks. She stated that what was unthinkable was for that man to get off scot-free and innocent, because of the horror of what he had done. Another victim named Brenda Aldred, a retired lady from Manchester, declared, "I am enraged to see someone like that allowed to live in Britain when he should never have been admitted to this country, and there he is today among us. I believe that he should be deported without delay." Ghannouchi, who was sentenced to hard labor in Tunisia for taking part in that attack, lives alternately at various secret locations in the north and east of London, a presence that is strongly deplored by all the British victims. The paper concluded by saying that none of them had been asked their feelings.

[18]One very charming approach I am acquainted with in political analysis is that which draws a parallel between the management of government and the management of institutions, between political efficiency and economic efficiency. Systems are compared and preferred on the basis of their ability to manage resources, which are naturally limited, especially in nascent democracies, and to make the best use of them for the public good in terms of cost-effectiveness and profitability. see **Ilchman, W.** and **Uphoff,** in *Le changement politique à la lumière de l'analyse économique (Political Change in the Light of Economic Analysis),* Trans., Paris, Tenances Actuelles, 1975.

[19]The Italian newspaper *La Republica* reported the speech.

[20]Léonid Albakine, Director of the Institute of Economics at the Academy of Science, spoke of a necessary period of transition, going from 10 to 20 years.

[21]See Jean Ellenstein, *D'une Russie à l'autre, op.cit.,* p. 634.

[22]*Ibid.,* p. 669.

[23]One strange paradox is that not just the total political liberalization, but also the rules of the political game, such as the electoral system, served the extremist opposition. To show that, one need only look at the results of the first stage of legislative elections. The Islamic Salvation Front carried 81% of the seats (188 out of 231 seats) with just 47.26 % of the votes. The ruling party, the National Liberation Front, only managed 6% of the seats (15 seats) with 23.38 % of the votes. Other parties were crushed as they carried no seats. Independents won just 3 seats, whereas the total proportion of the vote they obtained was almost 22%.

[24]Numerous commentaries have been written on the political changes in Algeria. Some have been marked by ignorance of the reality of life in Algeria. Some have been motivated by deep-seated hatred for this brotherly country. However, the most insightful are those written by Algerians themselves. Here are some examples, by no means exhaustive: A special edition of the magazine *Les temps modernes*, numéro spécial, "Algérie, la guerre des frères" ("Algeria, The War of Brothers"), January 1995. On Algeria itself, see also **Allonache, Merzek** and **Colonna, Vincent,** *Algérie 30 ans. Les enfants de l'indépendance (Algeria 30 years. The children of independence),* Paris, Ed. Autrement, 1992. **A group of authors,** *L'Algérie aujourd'hui (Algeria Today),* Paris, Ed. Paris Plus, 1992. On Islamic movements and their organization, see **Touati, Amine,** *Algérie. Les Islamistes à l'assaut du pouvoir (Algeria. Islamists in Assault on Power),* Paris, L'Harmattan, 1994.

[25]One can compare such regimes with the regimented societies Michel Crozier argues for in his anlysis of bureaucratic systems: **Crozier, Michel,** *La société bloquée (Regimented Society),* Paris, 1987.

[26]The most convincing theory of democracy, in our belief, is the one put forward by Robert Dahl in the early 1950s, where he says: "Pure original democracy cannot be reached through the same route as ideal economic competition." At its best, democracy takes on the form of a "polyarchy," literally the government of the many. **Dahl, Robert,** "A Preface to Democratic Theory," Chicago, 1956. On the concept of democracy, and when is a regime democratic or not, see also: **Touraine, Alain,** *Qu'est ce que la démocratie? (What is Democracy?),* Paris, Fayard, 1994. On the variety of democratic systems, not necessarily limited to one model, such as the one known as the Westminster model, see **UNESCO,** *Le temps de la démocratie (The Times of Democracy),* RISS no. 128, May 1991. In particular, see Guy Hermet's presentation of a critical theory of traditional criteria for democracy (citizenship, justice, the idea of the contract, participation, the law and order state), in: **Bidet, Jacques,** *Les paradigmes de la démocratie (The Paradigms of Democracy),* Paris, PUF, 1994. For a review of the history of democratic systems and anti-democratic regimes, see **Berstein, Serge,** *Démocratie, Régimes autoritaires et totalitarismes au 20e siécle (Democracy, Authoritarian regimes and Totalitarianism in the 20th Century),* Paris, Hachette, 1994; and also: **Duhamel, Olivier,** *Les Démocraties (Democracies),* Paris, Seuil, 1993.

[27]Cf. **Almond** and **Verba,** *The civic culture,* op. cit.

[28]See **Attali, Jacques,** *Les modèles politiques (Political Models),* Paris, PUF, 1992.

[29]See **Rupnik, Jacques,** "L'invention démocratique en Europe du Centre-Est," ("The democratic invention in Central-East Europe"), in **Minket Szurek** (ed.), op. cit., p. 51.

[30]*Elections fondatrices,* ("Founding Elections"), p. 56.

[31]In his November 7, 1988, address, one year into the Change, President Ben Ali said, "Our people are eager to turn over forever a painful and regretful page of our past, the page of feuds for power and conflicts for succession. Those protracted conflicts gave rise to forces of suspect constitution and relations, which were awaiting the opportune

moment to pounce on power, away from legitimacy, and in contempt of the will of the people."

[32]In this respect, we have adopted David Easton's model, which views a political regime from the perspective of its ability to control external factors, which are input to it, and to turn them into suitable output in the form of adequate decisions and actions which guarantee its stability and equilibrium at each stage by acting on the new factors. In my Ph.D. thesis of 1975, I had elaborated on how societies on the way to development (and pluralism) need to exercise greater control over inputs, to manage society strategically to serve the objectives of the regime, and to achieve a rapprochement between the demands and aspirations of the people and the political orientations devised by the government in a top-down fashion to achieve rapid development (and thereby to guarantee democracy, since there is an interdependence between the degree of development and that of political liberalization of any society). see **Chaabane, Sadok,** *Analyse stratégiste des processus de gouvernement dans les sociétés en transition (A Strategic analysis of the process of government in Societies in Transition)*, Tunis, Faculté de Droit, 1975.

INPUTS > > | INTERACTIONS OF THE POLITICAL REGIME | > > OUTPUTS

ENVIRONMENT   FEEDBACK

[33]See **Amami, Abdallah,** *The Nahdha Movement, Terrorist Organizations in the Islamic World: The Nahdha Model* (in Arabic), Tunis, STD, 1992.

[34]**Dunn, Michael Collins,** *Political Islam : The Case of Tunisia's al-Nahda,* Washington, The International Estimate, 1992, p. 105.

[35]Some of the most eminent writing on the subject includes **Amami, Abdallah,** op. cit. and the research done by **Allani, Alya,** *The Movement of the Islamic Tendency in Tunisia (1970-1987)* (in Arabic), Tunis, The Faculty of Humanities and Social Sciences, 1993. See also the research done by: **Ben Fdhila, Fatma,** and **Labidi, Najiba,** *The Islamic Movement in Tunisia: The Single Objective and the Double Talk* (in Arabic), Tunis, The Institute of Journalism, 1990. See also: **Charfi, Abdelmajid,** *Islam and Modernism* (in Arabic), Tunis, STD, 1991. And: **Al-Jorshi, Salah Eddine,** *The Islamic Movement in the Vortex* (in Arabic), Tunis, Dar al-Barraq, 1985. On the compatibility of democracy with religious regimes, see **Badie, Bertrand,** "Démocratie et religion," ("Democracy and religion"), in **UNESCO,** *Repenser la démocratie (Rethinking democracy)*, RISS, August, 1991, p. 129, who says that all religions are basically incompatible with democracy (p. 464). For a more in-depth analysis, see **Ben Achour, Iyadh,** "Islam et Laïcité," ("Islam and Secularism") in *Revue Pouvoirs*, No. 62, 1992, pp. 15-31. **Jeaît, Hichem,** in Collective Work, *Islam et politique au Proche Orient aujourd'hui (Islam and Politics in the Near East today)*, Paris, Gallimard, 1991. (In particular, cf. his study on the effects of the Gulf War).

For an outsider's view of Islam in major literature by eminent journalists, see **Balta, Paul,** *L'Islam et le monde (Islam and the World)*, Paris, Coll. La Mémoire du Monde, 1991. And by the same author:

Islam, civilisations et sociétés (Islam, Civilizations and Societies), Paris, Ed. Rocher, 1991.

[36]**Amami, Abdallah,** op. cit. p. 19.

[37]See "Rached Ghannouchi: The Face and the Mask," Tunis, Publications of the Agency of External Communications (ATCE), 1992.

[38]See **Amami, Abdallah,** op. cit. p. 175.

[39]The Islamic Liberation Party *(Hizb Al-Tahrir)* of Tunisia, is an offshoot of the original organization which was founded in 1952 in Jerusalem at the hands of Taqiyy Eddine Al-Nabhani, and then spread to Iraq, Kuwait, Lebanon, Syria, and Egypt. The organization also had a background in Europe, particularly in Germany, where it was joined by the Tunisian Mohamed Fadhel Shatara, who then returned to Tunisia, managed to mobilize some recuits, among whom was Mohamed Jerbi, who deputized for him at the rank of Commander, and set up the so-called "Accountable Committee", which is a structure that is created in countries where the party is still being started. The party knew a revival in the wake of the defeat of the pro-Nasser pan-Arab movement in 1967. Its real aim is to establish an Islamic Caliphate or theocracy throughout the Islamic world, with a crowned prince at its head. Members of the party in Tunisia, who were among those brought to trial, did not exceed 228.

[40]The Islamic Front *(Al-Jabha Al-Islamiyya)*, an offshoot of the Group for the Propagation of the Message, goes back to 1988. Mohamed Ali Harrath had founded it by meeting other partisans in the Al-Qasr mosque, near Souk Al-Asr in Tunis. The organizatio aims to establish an Islamic State, governed by *Shari'a* Law, and does not wish to stop at propagation and standing by watching the heretic government. On one Sunday in March 1988, the charter was laid down, a leading council was constituted, and Mohamed Khoja was appointed at the head of the council, with the rank of Prince. A regional council was also founded at Sfax, Tunisia, with Mohamed Khoja in charge of external communications. He was able to establish links with the Algerian Islamic Salvation Front, sending Tunisians through Annaba, Algeria, to the Peshawar region in Pakistan for military training and preparation for what they call Salvation Day. It later transpired that he had close ties with Rached Ghannouchi, that he had supervised training in Bosnia, under the cover of a humanitarian organization called "Reconciliation". Members of the Islamic Front in Tunisia did not exceed 120, who have all been brought to trial.

[41]The Movement for Social *Change (Harakat Al-Taghyyir Al-Ijtima'iy)* is an extension of the *Nahdha* Movement, which issued from it in the summer of 1990. On the surface, it differs from the *Nahdha* in not prescribing rules of individual conduct. For example, one is allowed to smoke or wear tights. Its *raison d'être* is to open wider horizons for recruitment, as a preparation for entry into the *Nahdha*. It was active in the region of Kebili. Ten of its members have been brought to trial.

[42]The Islamic Group *(Al-Jama'a Al-Islamiyya)* is an offshoot and a tributary of the *Nahdha*, with members mostly from the teaching profession. It specialized in social studies of the status quo and information gathering. Some of its trademarks include bilateral meetings in public places, cafés, and parks and the use of codes to pass on information. It was particularly active in the Mahdia region. Seven of its members have been brought to trial.

[43]The Group for Inquisition and Exile *(Jama'at Al-Takfir Wal-Hijra)* is a small splinter faction of the Islamic Front, and yet another tributary of the *Nahdha*. Led by Hassan Al-Haramiy, the group called for declaring the government to be heretical unbelievers *(takfir)*, for refusal to talk to it, and for emigration into Afghanistan to train to use weapons for a confrontation with the regime with the aim of building the Islamic State. All 25 partisans of the movement have been brought to trial.

[44]The Group for the Propagation of the Message *(Jama'at Al-Da'wat Wal-Tabligh)* remains active in Tunisia. Many of its members are ex-members of the *Nahdha*. It is one of the *Nahdha's* tributaries, as it lays the spiritual groundwork for it. Its acceptance by the

authorities is based on its rejection of violence. However, the political repercussions of that in feeding the theocractic movement are obvious. Seventy of its members, from the Ariana region, have been brought to trial for breaking the law on meetings, despite being ordered not to do so.

[45]The Martyr's Movement is, in our belief, now defunct following the trial of the one person who founded it, who was someone by the name of Abderrazak Hammami. He was under the influence of Khomeini's speeches and defined his movement as an Islamic organization for popular resistance against the evil ruling regime for the establishment of an Islamic State.

[46]The Disciples of the Truth *(Shu'bat Al-Haqq)* was founded by Samia Mannai, who calls for repentance and turning to the truth. It counted in its membership women who were in regular attendance at the Zeitouna Mosque. Some believe that this was a group set up by the *Nahdha* to recruit women. It was conspicuous for advocating the long black dress to cover the whole face, hands, and body for women, as well as the shaved head for men. Fourteen of its members from the Ben Arous and Tunis areas have been brought to trial.

[47]See below in the section on the Third Challenge. Ninety-one of its members have been brought to trial.

[48]Such organizations are thought to be part of a limited movement. At one time, they were active in certain universities, colleges, and trade unions. Thirteen Revolutionary Marxist Communists and 37 members of the pro-Libyan Arab Revolutionary Committees have been brought to trial.

[49]There are numerous references on the subject. We will just mention two: **Jazi, Dali,** *Les rapports entre l'Etat et le citoyen dans la Tunisie indépendante (State-Citizen Relations in Independent Tunisia)*, Ph.D. Thesis, Paris II, 1982. See also: **Omar, Abdelfattah,** *A Compendium of Constitutional Law* (in Arabic), Tunis, The Centre for Studies, Research, and Publication, 1987.

[50]On this phenomenon, which particularly is found in one-party regimes, see **Gaxie, Daniel,** *Les professionnels de la politique (Professionals in Politics)*, Paris, PuF, 1973. And also: **Mayer, N.** and **Perrineau, P.,** *Les comportements politiques (Patterns of Political Conduct)*, Paris, A. Colin, 1992.

[51]The bases of economic development are indeed political. see **Holt, R,** and **Turner, J.,** *The Political Basis of Economic Development : An Exploration in Comparative Political Analysis,* Trans. in Tendances Actuelles, Paris, 1970.

[52]The reader must recall the situation in Tunisia in the mid-1980s, when economic and social conditions were ripe for the emergence of marginalization and extremism, with an economic collapse compounded by social frustration, what with "a decrease in the value of the dinar, the bankruptcy of the government treasury, the closure of factories, the phenomenal rise in unemployment, the imposition of exorbitant increases in prices, and a swelling in the number of young people turned out on the streets."

[53]See the *Annual Report on Human Rights in Tunisia* (in Arabic), published by **The High Commission for Human Rights,** 1992. See also **Al-Ahmadi, Abdallah,** *Human Rights and Public Liberties in Tunisian Law* (in Arabic), Tunis, Orbis Impression, 1993.

[54]**Association Tunisienne de Droit Pénal,** *L'instruction (Pretrial Investigation)*, Seminar Proceedings, Manuscript, Tunis, 1992. Notably the paper by **Bel Haj Hammouda, Ajmi,** "Le silence de l'inculpé" ("The Silence of the Accused"). **Zine, Mohamed,** *Les droits de l'homme et les garanties de l'accusé dans le droit pénal (Human Rights and the Defendant's Right to Silence in the Penal Code)*, Tunis, ATCE, 1992.

[55]See **United Nations Publication,** "United Nations Work in the Field of Human Rights". On human rights in Arab countries, see especially: **Al-Basyouni, Mahmoud Sharif,** *Human Rights* (Two volumes), Beirut, Dar Al-'Ilm Lil-Malayin, 1989.

[56]Hassib Ben Ammar, President of the Institute, has made the point on more than one occasion. The Institute, which receives substantial financial backing from the Presidency, enjoys complete freedom in organizing conventions and events and has rendered invaluable services in disseminating the concepts and culture of human rights in the Arab world.

[57]No opinion polls have been conducted on this point. However, within the Social Research Agency, a private institution for social surveys and studies, Aziza Medimegh has carried out important research whose results point to that trend in Tunisian public opinion.

[58]See this reference in jurisprudence: **Sarsar, M. Chéfik,** *Le cadre juridique des partis politiques en Tunisie (The Juridical Framework for Political Parties in Tunisia),* Postgraduate Research Project, Faculté de Droit, Tunis, 1990.

[59]see **Ltayef, Shokri,** *Islamists and Women: The Oppression Project* (in Arabic), Bayram Publishing, Tunis, 1988. Numerous other articles have been written on women's achievements in Tunisia. See particularly an excellent collection of texts and figures on women's rights and their social and political situation in the series published on women by: **The Centre for Studies, Research, Documentation, and Information,** "Women of Tunisia. Reality and Prospects" (in Arabic), Tunis, 1995.

[60]We refer particularly to the *Declaration on the Eradication of all Forms of Fanaticism and Discrimination Based on Religion or Faith* by the United Nations General Assembly, on February 25, 1981. Following this legal requirement, international feeling was expressed through many recommendations of the Commission for the Prevention of Crime, where the principle has been adopted of incriminating the advocacy of hatred and instigation of fanaticism, to prevent movements doing this from claiming the cover of crimes of conscience.

[61]In his November 2, 1992, Carthage address, Ben Ali said, "Education and teaching in human rights are the best guarantees for the future and the key to a deeper awareness of them and to their integration in everyday life." See also the research article by: **J'i-dane, Riydh,** "The teaching of human rights in Tunisia," published in the *Human Rights Magazine,* The International Institute of Human Rights, Strasbourg, France.

[62]In his July 1, 1992, Carthage address, Ben Ali said, "The extremist religious movement, which is an extension of the international extremist religious network, has sought by terrorism and infiltration of republican institutions to wreak havoc and destruction. We are determined to combat it, because sedition and the backward ideas it would spread fly in the face not only of our democratic choice, but also of the very Islamic principles and values it claims to defend."

[63]**Ben Hamda, Abdelmajid,** "Religious Achievements in Tunisia the New Era" in joint work, *November 7, A Quiet Revolution* (in Arabic), Abdulkarim Ben Abdallah Publishing, 1992, 204 pages.

[64]That is the difference between Sunni and Shi'a. Sunnis do not believe there are mediators in Islam, because man's relationship with God is a direct one, whereas Shi'ites regiment that relationship, with theologians acting as the mediators. Since the Islamic Group was set up in 1972 in Tunisia, a number of articles have been published in the paper *Al-Ma'arifa (Learning)* trying to narrow the gap. In Edition No. 4, Volume V, Ghannouchi states that in Islamic history reform movements have been "the work of individuals," based on the personality of the reforming scholar, and on the legitimacy

of the regimes in power. Now, "the reforming attitude is not enough, for the whole house has come tumbling down, and therefore calls for new foundations." He then adds that he is "a disciple of three advocates, El-Banna, El-Mawdudi, and El-Khomeini" and that "the first leader who saw the potential of the idea of organization and connected it to the idea of founding an Islamic state was Imam El-Banna. He is the first Sunni reformer who introduced the idea of organization..."; and therefore he declares his adoption of the ideas of clandestine operation. The *Nahdha* then broke away from the Sunni Zeitouna Movement (led by Habib Mistawi and later Abdelkader Salama) and expelled leaders of the Movement for Enlightened Progressive Islam, particularly Hamida Enneifar, and Salah Eddine Al-Jorshi, appealing to special dispensations by Mahmoud Chaltout to bring closer the divergent schools and consecrate Sunni rituals of worship as Shi'ite Imamate theological practice. Partisans of the movement were then schooled in this Shi'ite doctrine, which was reinforced by Khomeini's victory.

[65]On May 22, 1991, Abdallah Kallel, Minister of the Interior, held a detailed news conference on these intrigues. He described the new organizational structure of the movement and the special wing, and listed the names of the ringleaders. This is documented in M. Dunn, *op. cit.*

[66]Publication of the paper was outlawed in January, 1991.

[67]Legally, it would have been possible to ban outlawed political parties from standing in the elections on independent lists. However, this course of action was rejected by Ben Ali, who preferred to leave open the way for a participation by all persuasions in the elections, through the independent ballots, which successive electoral amendments have left untouched as a way out to the extremist movements, and a gauge of their strength.

[68]See also: **Keddie, Nikki R.** "The Islamist movement in Tunisia," in *Maghreb Review,* Vol. 11, No. 1, 1986. **Lamhichi, Abderrahim,** *Islam et contestation au Maghreb* (*Islam and Dissension in the Maghreb*), Tunis, 1989. *Jeune Afrique,* "Ghannouchi: ce qui'il a dit à la police," ("Ghannouchi, What He Said to the Police") No. 1396, October 7, 1987.

[69]Says Ben Ali in this respect: "November 7 has restored sovereignty to the people. That means the country's destiny is now squarely on the shoulder of each and every one of the people" (November 7, 1989, address). See also: **Rustow, Dankwart A.,** "Democracy: A Global Revolution?" in *Foreign Affairs,* 69: 4 (Autumn 1990), pp. 75-90.

[70]In a speech on May 1, 1988, President Ben Ali said, "Much as the state works to guarantee a highly evolved modern political life, it must remain firmly fortified. We will spare no effort in strengthening its position, and raise its voice above all others."

[71]The Minister of the Interior issued instructions and circulars to revise provisions relating to the treatment of arrestees and the penalties attached to any abuse. On December 16, 1991, he promulgated Circular No. 895 enjoining chiefs of police stations to display, in their offices, the text of the vow taken by Interior Security officers before embarking on their duties. The circular reads thus: As a reminder to all Interior Security personnel and officers of the text of the vow specified in Article Six of Act No. 70 of 1982, dated August 6, 1982, enacting the General Statute of Interior Security forces, it is hereby made mandatory for chiefs of police stations and analogous active units attached to the various corps to display the aforementioned vow, a copy of which is transmitted to you in appendix via the relevant offices under the supervision of all the Directors General, who are hereby charged with the follow-up on the implementation of this procedure." Circular No. 904 on the publication of the United Nations Code of Conduct for Law Enforcement Officers, issued on December 24, 1991, by the Minister of the Interior reads thus:

In the context of the policies of Tunisia in the New Era in the area of democracy and the protection of human rights,

Considering the vital role played by Interior Security staff in spreading among citizens a sense of freedom and responsibility, of the safeguard of one's privacy and property, and of the protection of one's dignity and full rights,

In the belief that the protection of society and of its achievements and stability can only be discharged through the protection of the individual and of his privacy and dignity, through enhancing his awareness of his responsibilities in participating in the protection of society and its lofty ideals as well as in achieving its stability and prosperity,

In order to empower Interior Security staff to carry out their noble mission to the best of their ability,

I call upon all of them to follow to the letter the United Nations Code of Conduct for Law Enforcement Officers, to make of that Code the basic guidelines to abide by in the fulfillment of their duties, and to promote the respect of that Code on as wide a scale as possible.

Display of this Circular in all police stations and National Guard barracks is hereby made mandatory.

[72]Circular No. 72 on the signing of the commitment to respect human rights and public liberties, promulgated on February 24, 1992, by the Minister of the Interior:

In the context of promoting awareness among Interior Security officers and personnel of Tunisia of provisions on human rights and of international covenants to which Tunisia is a signatory, and in order to guarantee the communication of those provisions to all the Directors of Security Units in the various specializations, all Directors General and Directors in charge of Interior Security staff structures are hereby kindly ordered to oversee the signing of the appended agreement by all Interior Security officers and personnel the moment they are appointed to positions of leadership, starting from the position of Chief of Police Station, or an analogous post.

Agreement

To abide by human rights and public liberties

I the undersigned:_____

Name and Sumame: _____

Number: _____

Rank: _____

Attached to (1) [Corps]__ (2) Position___(3) [Stationed at]_____

In charge of_____

Hereby declare having taken cognizance of all Tunisian legislation and provisions relating to human rights and public liberties, and of all the international covenants to which Tunisia is committed in this respect.

Signature: _____ Date: _____

[73]There is a danger that must be exposed, which is the excessive pressure brought to bear by human rights organizations on governments facing difficulties from extremist movements. The pressure, centering around conditions of arrest, investigation, and trial, may push these governments to resort more readily to other methods of treatment for the members of those movements following their arrest, thereby avoiding any of the forms of harassment they usually face throughout the subsequent security and judicial stages. Indeed, some governments seem to have had recourse to such measures. Never has Tunisia done so. Never has she felt the need to do so.

[74]See **The High Commission for Human Rights,** *Annual Report* (in Arabic), Tunis, 1992.

[75]Among such terrorist laws there are, in France, Act No. 1020/86, dated September 9, 1986, supplementing the French Penal Code, and Act No. 541/87, dated July 16, 1987; in Britain, the Emergency Act on Northern Ireland of 1991; in the USA, Act No 399/99, dated August 27, 1986, and its amendments; in Egypt, Act No. 97 of 1992; and in Algeria, Decree No. 03/92, dated September 30, 1992. Switzerland has followed Tunisia's suit in promulgating a law for the criminalization of racial and religious discrimination enacted on June 18, 1993.

[76]See **General Assembly Resolution No. 49/147, dated December 23, 1994,** on the provisions and measures required for the prevention of all modern forms of racial discrimination and segregation, and of attendant fanaticism and intolerance. See also its other **Resolutions** on the same date, **No. 49/188,** on the elimination of all forms of religious intolerance, and **No. 49/213** on the United Nations Convention on Tolerance. See also **General Assembly Resolution No. 49/185,** dated December 23, 1994, on human rights and terrorism. For **the Ninth United Nations Conference on the Prevention of Crime in Cairo (April 29 to May 8, 1995),** see Egypt's proposal on relations between terrorism and organized crime **(A/CONF/169L.12/Rev1).** See also **the Declaration and Agenda Adopted by the Vienna International Conference on Human Rights (June 14-25, 1993),** and **the Tunis Declaration in the Regional Africa Convention** held in preparation for the International Conference of Human Rights (November 2-6, 1992).

[77]What is meant here is the extremist left, which some call leftism.

[78]Basically, former Prime Minister Mohamed Mzali and former minister Mohamed Sayyah, though for different reasons. See earlier paragraphs.

[79]Ben Jaballah, Hamadi, "Educational Reform and the Human Values Epic," in joint work, *November 7, A Quiet Revolution* (in Arabic), Abdulkarim Ben Abdallah Publishing, 1992, p. 354. Reform was entrusted to three bodies: The Supreme Council for Education and Higher Education, in charge of developing the major policies and assessment; the High Commission for Educational Reform, in charge of planning, coordination, and follow-up; the Sectorial Committees and the Ad-hoc Committees, in charge of proposing changes and reforming syllabi so as to best serve the new orientations of the regime. The committees, set up in April 1989, comprise, besides scholars and educational staff, representatives of political parties and trade unions and other parties to the National Pact. It is noteworthy that the Sectorial Committees covered very precise subjects such as philosophy, Islamic education, and music classes, with the aim of affording the student a wide-ranging education that raises the young in noble values and gentlemanly conduct. The Ad-hoc Committees covered such administrative areas as the educational organizational structure, make-up exam schemes, documentation and archiving, student assessment, teacher training, school vacations, careers and courses guidance, etc. The constitution of these committees has undergone changes so as to fulfill their mission to the best of their ability and without replacing the right-wing, fundamentalist movement by another extremist, left-wing movement.

[80]See **Kefi, Faiza,** Le droit à l'éducation et l'enseignement des droits de l'homme (The Right to Education and the Teaching of Human Rights), Tunis, ATCE, 1992.

[81]In his May 1, 1990, address, Ben Ali said, "There could be no development without democracy, no democracy without development. Democracy, much as it may be a value in itself, is a means that acquires its value from its effectiveness in allowing issues to be raised and addressed."

[82]Ben Ali's view of democracy is characterized by focusing on its motivational influence on human resources and its kindling of a sense of patriotism and pride in participa-

tion. In his November 3, 1988, address, he said, "We are firm in the belief that democracy is the ideal climate for the promotion of talent, skill, and creativity inherent to our people, and that it is the best means to put that creative talent at the service of the nation."

[83]In his July 19, 1988, address, Ben Ali said, "Tunisia today, having entered the stage of balanced political liberalism, is called upon to free economic initiative too, away from sectarian slogans and alluring promises." That balance between political and economic liberalism is what characterizes Ben Ali's orientation in the new era.

[84]**The Democratic Constitutional Rally,** summer school, 1994.

[85]See **Anderson, Lisa,** "Politics and Democracy," in *Government and Opposition,* 1990. Earlier, in his July 29, 1988, address, Ben Ali had said, "We would like our project to be a major incentive and motivation for consensus in the context of a national pact, marked by a pluralist content, by a democratic approach, and by moral support for the efforts to address the country's conditions and achieve its ambitions."

[86]National pan-Arab feeling has moved most Arabs. However, the manipulation by certain pan-Arab leaders of that feeling and their desire to impose their view of an Arab union, were what hindered that union and made many governments wary of domination and the exploitation of pan-Arabism for other ends. That is in fact what motivated Bourguiba's attitude to Nasserism and Baathism, as well as the support he got from the national elites in his party and in the left. It now is evident that pan-Arabism is on the wane, as a recent survey carried out by the Social Research Agency, 1993, reveals that to the question: "What is the top priority for you?", only 11.2 % answered it was the Arab nation, 14.7 % the Islamic nation, and 68.2 % placed Tunisia on the top of their list. Note that in Tunisia there is a confusion between Arabism and Islam, and that the 14.7 % does not mean support for fundamentalism.

[87]This case is a perfect illustration of the analyses made of closed societies, such as those by Mills, Mosca, Pareto, Burnham, etc. The most impressive portrait of regimented societies is that painted by **Michel Crozier** in his book *La société bloquée (Regimented Society), op. cit.*

[88]See **Ben Miled, Slim,** *La présidence á vie de la république(Presidency of the Republic for Life),* Tunis, Faculté de Droit, 1985; and **Ltayef, Mondher,** *Presidency of the Republic in Tunisia* (in Arabic), Tunis, Faculté de Droit, 1993.

[89]There is a wide choice of works on Parliament in Tunisia. As a sampling, we will just cite: **Omar, Abdelfattah,** *A Compendium of Constitutional Law* (in Arabic), *op. cit.;* and **M'daffar, Zouheir,** *Constitutional Law and Political Institutions,* Tunis, The Research Centre at the National School of Administration, 1992.

[90]A classic reference on this point is: **Moore, Clement Henry,** *Tunisia since Independence, 1965.*

[91]Derisory folk songs, now just coming to the surface in this era of the Change, used to parody the conduct of the State Prosecutor at that time. One such song goes thus: "Hey, hey, hey, Majda's in jail, hey, Majda's in jail, what a story they say...", in lament at the tragedy of an arrested person called Abdelmajid (nicknamed Majda). The song was dramatized in the play *Bunni, Bunni* by **Fadhel Al-Jaziri** and **Samir Al- Agrebi.**

[92]That step confirmed Ben Ali's words on April 9, 1991, when he said that he placed "human rights and basic liberties foremost among our principles and objectives, because of our belief that man will take no pride in belonging to his country, will have no part in social action, will not partake of the lofty ideals and noble goals of the nation, until his opinion is valued, his rights are respected, and his dignity is honored." That stance applies to all the national elites, democratic parties, and associations,

which, in the wake of the Change, have all acquired an unshakable sense of patriotism, and have no time for those who would sow skepticism over Tunisia's achievements.

[93]Berteji, Brahim, *La gratuité de la justice (Justice, Free of Charge)*, Tunis, Faculté de Droit, 1989.

[94]The General Monitoring Service of the Ministry of Justice is in charge of keeping a schedule of the cases of arrestees pending trial, and of notifying the relevant courts of cases where custody has exceeded three months.

[95]References abound on the constitutionality of laws, given the significance of the issue. We need only cite the following: **Ben Achour, Rafi'**, "Verification of the Constitutionality of Laws" (in Arabic), in *Mélanges Mzioudet*, Tunis, Faculté de Droit, 1994, pp. 82-7. **M'daffar, Zouheir,** *Le Conseil Constitutionnel tunisien (The Tunisian Constitutional Council)*, Toulouse, Presses de l'IEP, 1995. See also: **Ga'loul, Mtir,** *Guarantees of the Supremacy of the Constitution in Tunisia* (in Arabic), Tunis, Faculté de Droit, 1994.

[96]One exciting work on democracy is: **Menyahan, John A.,** *Learning Democracy, Memoirs of a University Lecturer* (in Trans.), Amman, Dar Al-Bashir, 1993

[97]Since the Administrative Court started its consultative mission in 1974 until August 31, 1995, it has offered 6,671 consultations. Annual figures have shown a steady increase from 312 in 1988, to 380 in 1990, to 494 in 1990. Experience has shown that the President abstains from issuing any orders which the court finds incompatible with current legislation. In fact, he recommends the same principle for the enactment of any other laws. From 1975 to August 31, 1995, the Administrative Court received 8,018 cases, of which 5,093 were petitions for the abrogation of an administrative decision, 854 were petitions for the suspension of an administrative order, 2,076 sought to appeal a judicial decision, and 1,664 were cassation cases. The number of cases has risen in the last four years to around 600 cases a year.

[98]**Tarchouna, Lotfi,** "L'institution du médiateur administratif en Tunisie" ("The Office of Commisioner for Administration in Tunisia"), in *Mélanges Mzioudet*, Tunis, Orbis Impression, 1994, pp. 201-325.

[99]See the earlier, introductory remarks.

[100]See particularly: **Sartori, Giovanni,** *Parties and Party Systems,* Cambridge, Cambridge University Press, 1976; and **Seiler, D.L.**, *Les partis politiques (Political Parties)*, Paris, A.Colin, 1993.

[101]See the newspaper *As-Sahafa*, 12 August 1994.

[102]See the journal *Pouvoirs*, Volume I, *L'alternance (Changeover)*, 1977.

[103]Details of all these organizations can be found in **the High Commission for Human Rights,** *Annual Report* (in Arabic), 1992. See also: **Blibech, Fadhel,** *Les associations (Associations)*, Tunis, Faculté de Droit, 1993.

[104]In his March 31, 1988, address, Ben Ali said, "We have drawn up a National Pact, which has so united all sectors and intellectual and political persuasions around its substance and common immutable values as to allow us to face the coming difficulties as one man."

[105]See **Ben Youssef Charfi, Salwa,** *La Ligue Tunisienne pour la Défense des Droits de l'Homme (The Tunisian League for the Defense of Human Rights)*, Faculté de Droit, 1987.

[106]Ben All has often recalled his words on February 3, 1988, when he said: "Our country is facing conditions which have piled up for years, armed with nothing but the few material resources at its disposal, and the potential of its children, who have done us proud, to shape a better future." That testified to a realistic assessment of the political regime's abilities. There were institutional, mobilizational, and material resources, and there was an ability to rally the active elites to guarantee the success of the desired societal project.

[107]This view coincides with Almond and Powell's approach in assessing the potential of political regimes. see **Almond, G.** and **Powell, B.**, *Comparative Politics. A Developmental Approach,* op. cit.

[108]Says Ben Ali, "Our nation's independence, our territorial integrity, our country's sovereignty, our people's prosperity, are a responsibility which rests with all Tunisians. The love, defense, and exaltation of one's country are the sacred duties of every citizen." (November 7, 1987, address).

[109]One leading analysis of political culture is that advanced by Robert Dahl in: **Dahl, R.,** *L'avenir de l'opposition dans les démocraties (The Future of the Opposition in the Democracies),* (Trans.), Paris, Laffont, 1966. On the political culture required for democracy and the concept of citizenship, see **Hermet, Guy,** "Présentation: Le temps de la démocratie?" ("Time for democracy?"), UNESCO, RISS, p. 267. In relating democratic changes in the history of France, Hermet notes how the rural population did not understand what went on in Paris: he reports them as wondering who was Republic, was it a lady who had replaced the King in Paris? On the cultural requirements of democracy, see **Hermet, Guy,** "Culture et démocratie" ("Culture and democracy"), UNESCO, 1993. On political education and integration, see **Percheron, Annick,** *La socialisation politique (Political Socialization),* Paris, A. Colin, 1993.

[110]**Lipset, Seymour Martin,** *Political man,* Baltimore, John Hopkins University Press, 1981. Lipset states, "The stability of democracy requires a moderate degree of friction between opposed political forces" (p. 78). See also: **Diamond, Linz J.** and **Lipset, S.,** *Les pays en développement et l'expérience de la démocratie (Developing Nations and the Experience of Democracy),* Paris, Nouveaux Horizons, 1993, pp. 23-30.

On nascent democracies see **Weffort, Fransisco,** "Les démocraties nouvelles, Analyse du phenomène," ("New Democracies, An Analysis of the Phenomenon"), in **UNESCO,** *La sociologie politique comparative (Comparative Political Sociology),* RISS, No.136, March, 1993.

[111]Besides previous references, see **Pye, L.** and **Verba, S.** (ed.) *Political Culture and Political Development,* Princeton, 1965. **Rosenbaum, A.,** *Political Culture,* New York, 1975. For a synopsis of studies on political culture, see **Schartzenberg, R. G.,** *Sociologie politique (Political sociology),* Paris, Montchrétien, 1978.

[112]**Barrour, Emmy,** in **Gresh, Alain** (ed.), *A l'Est, des nationalismes contre la démocratie,* op. cit. p. 114.

[113]At the head of this organization presides a Central Committee of 83 members and a Political Bureau of 13 members. The party, with a five-part organization (one unemployed person, one worker, one student, one pupil, and one head of an organization), has some presence in the coastal Govemorates (Gabes, Sousse, Bizerta), Greater Tunis, Siliana, Le Kef, and Jendouba, as well as a presence in some universities and colleges, which is noticeably shrinking, and in such trade unions as the secondary school teachers' union, the postmen's union, and the railroad and transport unions. Since 1992, its presence has been on the wane in the central trade union and in associations. It has disappeared from universities.

[114]**Francis Fukuyama,** Op. cit. p. 71.

[115]Following the municipal elections, a statement issued by **the Renewal Movement** on June 5, 1995, asserted the need for "working to build a strong, united, and progressive democratic movement."

[116]**Chaker, Mustapha,** *Histoire du Parti Communiste Tunisien (A History of the Communist Tunisian Workers' Party),* Postgraduate Research Project, Paris, 1972.

[117]See **Al-Fitouhi, Wafa Al-Khalifi,** *The Progressive Socialist Rally and the Unionist Democratic Union* (in Arabic), Postgraduate Research Project, Tunis, Faculté de Droit, 1995.

[118]Cf. The Rally's Statute as well as the programs of its conferences, which have generated a new political discourse for the Democratic Constitutional Rally to reflect Ben Ali's orientations in the different domains.

[119]See **Dahl, Robert,** *Modern Political Analysis, 1963* (Trans. *L'analyse politique contemporaine*), op. cit. It may be useful to recall the organizational structure that has been suggested for the classification of nascent democracies, on the basis of degree of consensus and participation of elites :

STRATEGIES

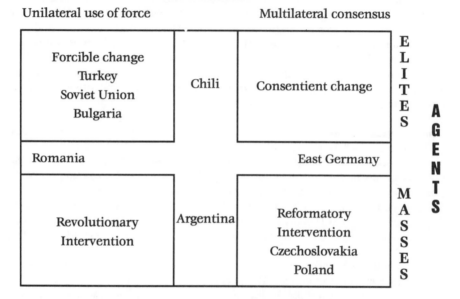

See **Karl, Terry Lynn,** and **Schmitter, Philippe,** "Les modes de transition en Amérique Latine," ("Modes of Transition in Latin America"), in **UNESCO,** *Le temps des démocraties en Europe du Sud et de L'Est (The Epochs of Democracies in Southern and Eastern Europe),* RISS, No.128, April 1991, pp. 285-302.

[120]In this book, we have not sought to present a review of political systems in Africa which have been forced to enter democracy through "National Congresses" with the participation of all political parties and persuasions, but with a quickening succession of events that have so rocked them as to unhinge their stability with the socialist summit held at La Baule, in 1990, ending in seven heads of state being unseated: Hissine Habre in Chad, Moussa Traore in Mali, Denis Sassou-Nguesso in the Congo, Matieu Kérékou in Benin, Didier Ratsiraka in Madagascar, Aristide Pareira in Cape Verde, and Pinto da Costa in São Tomé. The presidents of Rwanda and Burundi lost their lives. In Senegal, the elections of February 21, 1993, took place in a climate of fear that very nearly turned into a civil war. If we look at parties which have benefited from unconstrained liberalism, we find they number 260 parties for 40 million inhabitants in Zaire, 75 for 2.5 million in the Congo, 35 for 4.5 million in Benin, 50 for 7 million in Mali, 12 for 2 million in Mauritania, and 33 for 13 million in Madagascar. The President of Zambia stated that if he opened the way to all parties, he would have 73 par-

ties on his hands, one for each tribe. See **Lugau, Bernard,** *Afrique (Africa)*, Paris, Ed. Christian de Barbillat, 1975. See also *Jeune Afrique Economique,* "Les islamistes à l'assaut de l'Afrique Noire" ("Islamists in Assault on Black Africa"), No. 185, November 1994, pp. 101-109. And also: **Nguema, Issac,** "Violences, Droits de l'homme et développement en Afrique" ("Violence, Human rights and development in Africa"), in *Revue Juridique et Politique, Indépendance et Coopération (Independence and Cooperation)*, May 1995, pp. 121-132.

[121]The statement maintained that the municipal elections have shed light on "the future of pluralism and the parties," which "requires a radical and far-reaching solution." In particular, it asserted that "the national consensus has fulfilled its role in protecting the integrity and stability of the country, giving support to the national government in isolating the reactionary and mercenary movement, with the participation of the progressive [Renewal] Movement, which has not stooped to objection for the sake of opposition, nor to being associated with suspect alliances. However, the national consensus has not benefited all on an equal footing, and has in fact become unilateral, serving the interests of one party at the expense of the other democratic political parties, and other purposes than pluralism, and eventually being diverted from its original objectives." The statement insisted, "the contradiction between the culture of consensus and the culture of the opposition is evident, particularly during the elections, when parties which are a part of the consensus, which spread its culture, and which abide by its letter and spirit, find themselves in the elections called upon to engage the ruling party in an unequal struggle. Of little use is consensus then to them, with no means at their disposal to fight the electoral battle."

[122]In the municipal elections of 1995, on the ballots for the Democratic Constitutional Rally, 644 women were nominated out of 4,074 candidates. The presence of women in municipal councils has risen from 14% (1990) to 19% (1995). □

INDEX